Secrets of eBay

Secrets of eBay

Strategies and Tips Used by the Most Successful eBay Sellers

Donny Lowy

iUniverse, Inc.

New York Lincoln Shanghai

Secrets of eBay
Strategies and Tips Used by the Most Successful eBay Sellers

iUniverse, Inc.

For information address:
iUniverse, Inc.
2021 Pine Lake Road, Suite 100
Lincoln, NE 68512
www.iuniverse.com

ISBN: 0-595-30674-8

Printed in the United States of America

Preface

This publication is designed to provide accurate and authoritative information in regard to the subject matter covered. It is sold with the understanding that the author is not engaged in rendering legal, accounting, financial, investment, or other professional service. If legal advice or other expert assistance is required, the services of a competent professional person should be sought. The information in this book is only for educational purposes and should never be used unless one has first personally consulted with a licensed professional. By reading this book you are acknowledging that you could lose 100% of any money that you might decide to spend. You may read this book for entertainment or educational purposes but you should not use the information without the specific instructions of a professional who knows your personal situation.

Introduction

I will introduce you to a world that you have never experienced before. You might have heard of it in the media, but you might not have actually ever seen the potential of it. Now, for the first time, you will have an outstanding opportunity to actually make money from a phenomenon, which millions of people have been enjoying on a daily basis. Many more people have been using eBay to make a part-time and a full-time income from it. See, what makes eBay amazing is that it is simply visited by millions and millions of people *and* it is also a resource that any businessperson can use whether they have a one-person operation or a business with a thousand employees. The eBay site is a meeting point for thousands and thousands of different parties with many types of products and services who can instantly connect with other people who need their products and services—since you probably already realize, one of the challenging parts of a business is setting the correct price and marketing your services in a correct way. The eBay site helps you to instantly determine at what price your products will sell best and how to market your products.

You see, eBay is an auction and an auction operates by allowing people to set the bid at the price that they are willing to pay and the person with the highest bid wins the item. Now, you might wonder, I also mentioned that it helps people market properly, so how can eBay help to market your item properly? Once you list an item you will attract different peoples' attentions, who will look at the product and begin e-mailing you and you will see from their inquiries and based on the price that the bidding has reached, if you are doing a good job of actually marketing the product or not. If you are not doing a good job at marketing the product, you will know right away since you will see that you are not getting the price that you feel your product should go for or you might have realized that the product or service that you are trying to sell, does not have a market. You see, eBay can help you in many ways, it can help you find the best price to sell your product at, it can help you find what the best selling products are, and it can actually help you learn how to sell the product. You can also take a lot of the guesswork out of business by observing other peoples' auctions and seeing how they sell their products and services and what the best price is for the product you are selling.

There are many more facets on making money on eBay. Before you continue into the book, I would like to remind you that what makes eBay especially lucrative for people, is that you do not need to have high capital to start with or any sort of education or advanced degree. All you need to have is ambition, motivation and creativity which you can learn from the eBay auction process. So with that in mind, I invite you to start Chapter One and I hope that this book helps you immensely with all your endeavors on eBay!

Chapter 1

Many people wonder why now is the best time to start an eBay business and I will tell you that in a very concise and short statement. The best time is now, simply because there is plenty of money to be made. All you need to do to start an eBay business and to succeed is to find the right merchandise to sell, learn how to properly describe it, which means knowing how to market the merchandise, and simply buy it cheap enough so that when you sell it, you will be able to make a good profit. Now, there are many opportunities to find cheap merchandise on a daily basis and even more opportunities to *sell* that merchandise. As was mentioned in the introduction to this book, eBay is a meeting place that connects millions of people in one place. You will have an opportunity to sell almost any type of merchandise or service that you can imagine. Think of it, for every product there is a buyer and for every seller there is his or her counterpart waiting for him.

Through eBay, you will be able to discover millions of possibilities to sell your products and services. For instance, if you discover a special closeout at a going-out-of-business sale or if you go to an auction and find a really cheap price on a good line of merchandise, you can sell it on eBay. Once you learn how to properly describe the items, take pictures of the items, and to list the items correctly, then you will be able to find a good buyer for those products. For a product that you bought at an auction, where there were no interested buyers, you might find an interested buyer located on the other side of the country. For example, you might go to an auction at an ice cream store. That ice cream store might have some really good machinery to make chocolate soft ice cream, but in this case, the auction you attended could have been located in some small suburb out in your local city where there were no interested buyers for that particular type of machine. Now that does not mean that there are no interested buyers for that machine, it just means that there is no one in that area who is interested in that machine. However, there could be a small store on the other side of the country that might desperately want that machine and might be considering purchasing the same machine for the full wholesale price. Now, if you can offer them that same machine for a fraction of the price they were already planning to pay, then you will have an easy time selling that machine. Therefore, two elements go into successfully doing business. One is being able to locate the merchandise at a very good price and the other is knowing how to market that merchandise so people see the value of the item that you have and find a reason for buying it from you.

There are many opportunities to make money on eBay. Those opportunities are presenting themselves now in the changing economy. Think about every time you hear of a business opening or a business closing; these openings or closings present an opportunity for you. On the one hand, there is a lot of merchandise available and on the other hand, there will be many businesses that will need merchandise. What eBay allows you to do is to reach out to all those businesses looking for merchandise. You will also be able to reach out to all those businesses that need to get *rid* of their merchandise. Many successful eBay sellers constantly advertise that they are able to liquidate merchandise on eBay. If they find a small business that is going out of business, they let them know. "Hey look, I can sell your merchandise on eBay so you do not have to try to liquidate, have a going-out-of-business sale or spend the time meeting with different buyers who might or might not be interested." You could offer them a decent price to take all their merchandise and sell it at once.

You could also make it even easier for yourself by taking their merchandise on consignment. Consignment is where you take the merchandise, you do not pay up front for it, you make an agreement that you have a certain, specified amount of time to be able to sell that merchandise and once you sell that merchandise you will split the proceeds. Most consignment sales are done where a person can receive anywhere from 15 % to 50 % of the proceeds, depending on the final price of the merchandise. If someone were selling $1,000.000 worth of inventory, then it would be fair to the seller to keep 15 % of the proceeds. If, on the other hand, you are selling $5,000 or less, of merchandise, then you could see why a seller would insist on keeping 50 % of the proceeds for the work that he or she has done. They have put in a lot of work, energy and time; researched the product, discovered the best ways to sell that product, went through the time of answering e-mails and phone calls, and for all that work they are obviously entitled to receive a fair amount of the proceeds.

Now, there are many types of situations were you can make money using an eBay business. Remember, eBay is experiencing a tremendous amount of popularity now and for the foreseeable future as it continues to grow. The best time to get into any business segment is when it is strong and growing. This way you could learn eBay now, you could learn how to make money now and you could learn how to run your business properly; then as eBay expands and attracts more and more users, you will have experience in and will have learned how to and be ready, to sell. Think about it this way: Every type of business, like everything in life, has a learning curve to it; it takes a certain amount of time to learn how to properly work in a specific medium and how to get the most that you can, out of that medium.

It is not just a matter of waking up one day and deciding that you are going to do business in a certain market or field and that you are going to be very successful. Because, of course, you will make some mistakes in the beginning! You have to learn some things through trial and error, but eventually, God willing, you will be able to succeed and achieve your goal.

So, it is the same with eBay. You want to position yourself early in the business so you will be able to learn the ropes and, little by little, you will learn what mistakes to avoid, what things you need to do in order to be successful—you will learn your own tips and strategies that will enable you to *succeed*. You want to start *now*, this way. As more and more people join eBay and are looking for merchandise, you will be positioned in a way that you will know how to sell the merchandise instead of waiting for the future, and then having to learn later on how to start selling to those people. You could get the early stages out of the way now, learn how to sell and develop your skills, presently.

Remember, start small and begin learning how to run your business with a limited amount of money up front. Meaning, you do not want to make a large investment only to discover that you made a mistake and cannot sell the merchandise that you are sitting on. Instead, you want to start very small, you could actually list quite a few items on eBay and test it out for yourself. Buy ten or twenty dollars worth of merchandise; go to a garage sale, buy some nice looking pieces, an old painting or a few collectibles, go to a used book store and get some used books, negotiate a good price with the owner so that you can develop your buying and negotiating skills, you could even buy used C.D.s. Then you put that merchandise up on eBay, you write decent descriptions, take good, focused pictures of it, and then you will see what it takes to successfully sell that merchandise, while auctioning through different approaches.

Make sure to always give your contact information so that bidders can contact you. Once you have put that merchandise on eBay, you will discover through actually doing what you are learning, what it takes to make money by running these auctions.

Once you see exactly what you need to do and what steps you need to take to make money on eBay, then you can invest more money into your business by contacting a wholesaler to buy a larger amount of merchandise. You could even go to auctions and going-out-of-business sales and spend more money on merchandise because then you will know *what* kind of merchandise actually sells on eBay *and* you will know how to sell that merchandise.

Think about it, what better time is there to start a business—of course you all want to make money—but isn't the best time to start a business when you do *not* desperately need that money? If you currently have another source of income and you can start your business on the side, develop it at your own pace where you feel no pressure and you are not rushed to make money from it right away, then you are in an advantageous position. In a sense, you will be able to develop a second job without having to fully immerse yourself in that job. In other words, you will not have to jump into the ocean without first having to test the waters.

Many people who start franchises, restaurants, retail stores, or other types of businesses are taking a very big chance because they will never know how the business will work out until they actually open up their doors to the public. If the business does not work out, they are in big trouble because they have already spent ten or twenty-thousand dollars trying out the business. At that point, it will be too late to simply lock up the doors and try another business venture. While they cannot take that option and simply close their business if their business is not working out, they will never be able to recover the thousands of dollars they spent on their business.

On the other hand, when you look at your eBay business, you can start simply with a very small amount of money, have plenty of time to test the business, grow it as you go along, and you will always be able to keep your current income.

In fact, many people spend their evenings working on their eBay businesses. They still have their full-time jobs, they might be at school full-time, they might have an actual full-time business, or they might even have a retail store or restaurant. At night they come home, they take pictures of the merchandise they plan to put up on auction, write detailed descriptions for that auction, put up all the items on eBay and then they spend the rest of their evenings answering e-mails or returning phone calls and receiving the payments for their merchandise. They spend their weekends mailing out the merchandise. They could actually drop the items off at UPS or go to the post office during their lunch break, or they could spend one day a week taking care of all their shipping.

You could actually even have the shipping done straight from your house by having UPS come pick up the merchandise directly. UPS charges a small fee, which is quite insignificant when you are actually running your business and you look at the cost in terms of the proceeds that your business is returning. You could even take it one step further: You make eBay your main business because you realize that it is already growing to a point where you are suddenly at a large volume of shipments.

Whether you are sending out one package a day or a hundred, you could set up a UPS account that has a daily pickup option. That means that there will be a UPS truck stopping by your house once a day at a set time, dropping off packages to you and picking up packages from you. What you do is print out the label for UPS, using UPS software that UPS gives you. You print out those labels, put them on the box and you have the boxes ready at a set time. It could be early morning or late afternoon. UPS will come to you and pick up those boxes, and then you could return to your regular routine.

The eBay site has many advantages that other businesses do not have, such as: you do not have to meet customers face-to-face, you do not have to do any personal selling, and you do not have to stand by, waiting to answer customer inquiries. You can reply to people's e-mails on your own time and at your own convenience. You can answer phone calls at your own convenience, as well.

A store does not have that option; they have to be open when customers want to shop. Otherwise, they would not make any sales. Therefore, there are many reason's in favor of starting an eBay business. There will be many other reason's that will be personal to you. Perhaps you want to leave the current job you are in, maybe you are not happy with the level of income you have, or maybe you are a student who wants additional money to spend without having to take another job or having to get a part-time job. I know of some people who are retirees who use eBay to supplement their social security income. Again, there are many reason's why it is beneficial to make money with eBay and as you can see from reading articles in your local newspapers and magazines or even on the television, you will read, hear about, and see over and over, people's success stories, where they are making money on eBay, in the news.

Before you end this chapter, let me leave you with one more story. I recently spoke to an individual who has seven employees and sells a quarter of a million dollars of merchandise in a year. He specializes in selling computers that come off leases. Let us say there is a bank that has twenty machines and after three years of leasing the equipment they are done with the machines. Now the bank plans to buy brand new computers, they do not need those computers anymore so they return them to the leasing company. Now the leasing company has no use for those computers. They are in the business of leasing merchandise not of holding or stocking merchandise and, for sure, they are not in the business of selling used computers because their customers, such as the bank, who previously used the computers, are looking for brand-new merchandise.

Therefore, the individual that I met goes ahead and he purchases all the computers he can get his hands on from the leasing company. He makes sure, of course, that he can get a good price so he has a decent margin to make money.

Remember, he is working on volume, so he is more concerned with making a small profit per item by selling many pieces, than a higher profit by selling a few pieces at a more expensive price. If I could make a suggestion, that would be the route that I would suggest you take, especially in the beginning of your business.

Now, the individual who sells a quarter of a million dollars in computers does it all on eBay. He has a small office, located in the Northeast, specifically Massachusetts, and he does quite well at his business. Therefore, with this individual, who started from scratch and has seven employees, from looking at his auctions, I can *see* that he does quite well.

Think of how happy you would be if you could develop a business from scratch simply on eBay. This individual never has to make a cold call, never has to go on sales calls and meet at people's offices, never has to make any presentations; he simply buys the computers, which I am sure he does over the phone and might even be able to do it by e-mail. He has the computers sent to his warehouse, then he has his workers take pictures of the computers, write up descriptions, then pack up the computers. He puts up all the auctions on eBay, he answers e-mails and calls throughout the auction process, and then when he receives the payment from the bidders, he sends out these computers out—and his business is doing a quarter of a million dollars!

Let us assume that his profit margin is only 20%, which is $50,000 after all of his expenses. More realistically, since these leasing companies have no use for these computers—even though the computers might have a retail value of five-hundred dollars—the leasing company does not have the time or the capabilities to sell each computer to the retail market.

So since they essentially got most of their money back already by leasing the computers to the bank, they are happy to get rid of a five-hundred dollar computer for fifty dollars. Therefore, in the case of the man who sells the computers on eBay, his profit margin might even be as high as 90%. That means that $250,000 is returning approximately $220,000 a year, which is a lot of money!

Keep in mind that this individual started from scratch and that there are many other great stories. There are individuals who sell packing supplies on eBay for all the other eBay sellers who need to pack up their merchandise in boxes and send them out. They need to buy their packing supplies from *some*where. So, where else to buy them from, but directly from eBay where they make their own sales?

As you can see, there are many opportunities to make money on eBay and I believe that now is the best time—especially if you are trying to develop a business into new areas or are looking to start a business. People are becoming more used to buying merchandise, products or even paying for services directly on the internet. The eBay site is even better than an ordinary web site because eBay has a built-in market of millions of people who come to visit their web site every day looking for merchandise, products, and services. Why not involve yourself in eBay and become one of the sellers? Who would *not* take advantage of this great market?

With that, I will close this chapter. I invite you to spend some time before you continue into the next chapter brainstorming about what types of business you think would do well on eBay and how you could see yourself succeeding on eBay.

In the next chapter, I will discuss how to determine the best type of business for you to start on eBay. Before I do that, and before I give you my ideas and suggestions on how you can decide what the best business in your personal situation could be, you need to do some critical thinking.

I do encourage you to analyze some of the things in your life that are motivating you to start a business, because I believe that this thought process will also enable you to decide what *type* of business that you will be most successful at. By type of business, I do not mean where to sell or how to sell, because I think you can both agree that eBay is a very promising marketplace and a very lucrative lifestyle for you, depending, of course, on your own situation and abilities. I am referring to the type of business you want to develop on eBay, whether it is a retail business, wholesale business, antique business, collectibles business, or a service business. So with that, I'll end the chapter, let you do some thinking of your own, let you make some decisions, and let's get ready for chapter two.

Chapter 2

Many people ask me, "What are the best products to sell on eBay? Should I sell collectibles? Should I sell antiques? Should I sell clothing, books? Should I sell music?" That is of course, a good question. The answer to that question is extremely valuable because if you could know exactly what to sell on eBay, then of course you would already be halfway there. Then all you would need to do is to find that product and start selling it and if the answer to that question were really that simple, there would be many more successful people on eBay. Now, while the answer really is not that difficult to solve, I will very shortly come up with some suggestions and maybe a few good, solid answers to that question.

I want to remind you that there really is no right or wrong answer. You see, when you walk out out to your street and go to your nearest shopping mall, you walk in on the ground floor, then you go to the second floor and on up to the third floor, while you notice hundreds of different types of stores. Moreover, if you look through the phone book, you will see thousands of different retail businesses, hundreds of different wholesale and manufacturing businesses—you will even see many subcategories that exist within professions.

What I am trying to say is, there are many different routes you could take to make money on eBay. It would be very shortsighted to try to figure out only one business because in all actuality there are many ways to make money on eBay, and of course if you want to succeed, you need to start somewhere—so you need to start from step one. While you might end up branching out into other businesses in the long run, you need to begin from one point. If you make things too complicated from the beginning, you will end up having nothing. Yet again, it is important to keep the idea of more than one business in mind.

As you know, if you try to chase after too many opportunities, you will end up conquering none of those opportunities. On the other hand, if you focus on one opportunity, learn how to master that opportunity, learns what you need to do to achieve your goals, and put all of your energy into that goal, you will be able to succeed. It is the same with eBay. At some point in your business you will want to expand, or add more lines to your product and you will want to include other services, which you did not include before. I strongly recommend you only decide to focus on one line and even on one product within that line, especially at the beginning.

For example, if you wanted to sell socks on eBay, I recommend that you decide if you are going to sell dress socks or sports socks and within sports socks or dress socks you have to decide if you will be selling women's or men's socks. Then within those two categories, you can decide if you will be selling boy's socks or girl's socks. Alternatively, you could even decide to sell diabetic socks or dress socks for weddings. Whatever the category is, you need to be very, very specific and only focus on the one product. Once you decide what product it is that you want to sell, then you can research that market fully. You need to research every-thing about that market, asking questions such as, "Who are the retailers selling it if the wholesalers are selling it?" "Who are the customers that buy that item?" "What are the prices those customers expect to pay for the item?" "What is the most they will pay for the item?" and "What is the least they will pay for the item?" By least, I mean of course, everybody would love to save money and pay as little as possible, and there is a price that people are used to paying for it and if they see the price is too low, surprisingly, they will not buy the item because they assume there is something wrong with it.

If you are seeing a good, solid suit priced at $150. and you saw a store selling a similar suit for only fifty-dollars, I bet you would be very, very hesitant to buy that suit because you would assume there was something wrong with it, even though the suit would be 100 % fine. However, if you saw the suit that was nor-mally priced at $100., selling for $89, you might assume that they are having a good sale on the suit. On the other hand, instead of increasing the price of an item, you can sell even more of the same item. Let me give you an idea. For instance, there is a customer looking for a tuxedo for his son's wedding. Now, that customer knows that his son's wedding, hopefully, will only happen once. you know that today, the percentage is higher that it will happen more then once, but I won't get off on that topic. Therefore, this customer is looking for a tuxedo for his son's wedding. He looks at the tuxedos and sees one priced at $200., but then there is another tuxedo all the way in the left corner and its price is $300. The first thing that father will say to himself is, "There is got to be a reason why this tuxedo is priced so much higher then the other tuxedos!" Then he will go ask the salesperson, "How is this tuxedo made? Is it a better quality? Is the design nicer? Is this brand name a better brand name?"

Think about it, he wants to make sure for this great event in his life, in his son's life, that he will be dressed the best way he can be and he will be willing to spend more money for that. Sometimes, by finding the highest price, your customers will be willing to pay and by charging that price, you will be showing your customers that the item you are selling is distinguished from the rest of the items and it deserves to be sold and to be bought for that high price. You will end up selling more then the other items that sell for less, because they could be seen as having a lesser value.

I will get back to the topic I was discussing. Now you know that you need to focus on one product. You also know that once you find that product, you will want to research it fully, you will want to order catalogues provided by people who sell that product, contact wholesalers, you will want to contact retailers who sell that item, you will actually want to meet customers who buy and use that item. So more importantly now, how do you decide what item to sell? I mean, even if you look at socks, there are hundreds of different socks that you can buy. There are so many different designs and different manufacturers; there are so many countries you can get socks from. You do want to make sure that you are making the right decision with those items. So how can you know if the item you have decided to sell is going to be a good item or not? Even if you have the item, how do you know if people will actually buy it or not?

Remember at the beginning of the book I mentioned that you do not want to take a big chance at the beginning. You do not want to make a mistake in the beginning of your business and cut yourself short. You will have nothing, you will get discouraged and you will not continue. Instead, you want to take a slower approach and make sure at the beginning that you have the best odds at being successful. How can you decide what product will sell on eBay and how can you decide what product you should try selling on eBay? Guess what? You want to pick a product that you are intimately familiar with, as of now. That is right; you want to pick a product or service, if you decide to offer a service on eBay, that you currently and actively use, that you are very familiar with, something you could almost consider yourself an expert on.

Let me give you some ideas. If you are a mother of young children, you might want to sell products your children use. If you take your kids to Toy's R Us, maybe on a weekly or monthly basis, you will know exactly which toys your kids are interested in playing with. Then you could go ahead, purchase those toys on a wholesale basis, and offer them on eBay. You will have a very good chance of becoming successful because you will know exactly which toys kids like to play with and the prices their parents can be expected to pay—or if you can offer those products at a cheaper price then they pay for them at the store, then you have a good chance at selling them. Alternatively, let me say you are someone who enjoys fishing and you have been fishing for the last fifteen years. You know every tackle, every bait, the best rods to use; you know everything about fishing. You have had a subscription to a fishing magazine for the last four or five years, you watch the fishing channel, you love talking about fishing stories with your friends, you go on boat rides at least once a month and you know what? You are an expert in the fishing area. You need to go ahead and find one product within the myriad of products that a fisherman would use, take that product, and market it on eBay.

You find out who the wholesalers are and you decide if you want to buy it from the wholesaler or if you want to buy it from the manufacturer. Maybe you want to go to the retail store and buy their slow-moving merchandise. By marketing it properly, you could sell it to a customer on the other side of the country who actually might need that merchandise. You could even set up a joint venture, that I will discuss later, that allows you to gather with the manufacturer, the wholesaler, the distributor, or the retailer to sell their merchandise. You could even contact a friend of yours, a colleague, an associate or a relative who enjoys fishing with you, and even offer to help them sell their fishing equipment that they no longer use. Maybe they have upgraded their fishing equipment or maybe they have decided to take a break from fishing for a while. You could help them sell their equipment, their rods, their bait, their tackles, whatever they use for fishing. You could offer to sell it for them and you keep a commission on the sales. See, there are many, many ways to obtain merchandise. You might actually decide to implement every method for getting merchandise, in this way you will always have a constant flow of merchandise that you could continue to sell.

You build up your customer base; your customer base will know what to expect from you, what you offer, and they will always be checking your auctions, looking for merchandise. Again, that is another reason to focus on only one specific product line. You want people on eBay to know that your auctions are for a certain product or service. If they know you offer a certain product or service, they will always keep returning to your auctions to see what it is that you are offering this week. For instance, if you happen to love books from the early 1900s, and you discover that there is a seller on eBay who, every single week, offered twenty new books that he located at estate sales or garage sales and he offered these books from the early 1900s on auctions, on eBay every week. Wouldn't you love to follow every single one of his auctions and have the opportunity to win one of those books? Of course, you would! Same way here, if you love hard-to-find movies and there was a seller who was somehow able to get those movies and always offered them, on eBay, you would follow every one of his auctions until you were able to win one of the movies that he offered.

See, eBay allows bidders—who are the people who are actually looking at buying the merchandise—it allows them to sign up for a free service that helps them to keep track of different auctions by sellers. So they can be updated every time a certain seller offers merchandise the same way. On the other hand, you can always contact the people who are looking for that type of merchandise by allowing bidders to sign up for an e-mailing list and then you can contact them. Of course, this has to be done according to the eBay rules and you have to have the permission of the people you send e-mails. What you need to do in order to develop a following: In order for people to want to come to you and buy from you and to know what you are offering, you want to be very specific and specialize in one product just so you develop a name for yourself. Once you develop a name for yourself, your reputation will grow. People will know that you offer quality merchandise. Of course, always make sure to offer top-of-the-line merchandise so people will look forward to and be excited to buy from you.

Think about it, if once a week you put up an auction for a great item, and every week people will see the feedback that you receive from the top bidder. Remember there is only one winner for that item, only one top bidder who buys that item from you. In addition, feedback is information; it is a posting of the seller and the buyer who took part in the transaction. If I had bought something from your auction, I would post feedback on your name, it would say how I felt about the transaction and you would do the same under my name. Now I can read your feedback and you can read my feedback and see what comments were posted about each other. I could write that you did a great job in delivering the book, you packed it beautifully, you used shrink-wrap and a nice box, and it arrived on time. Then you could post a message regarding me on my account, of course; I appeared as the buyer, and you could say that "this buyer" did a great job with paying on time, the payment was received immediately and it was a pleasure dealing with "this buyer." Now other people will then want to work with us because they will see the good feedback that was received from other people. If you want to receive good feedback from people and you want other people to use that feedback, then you will benefit from offering merchandise that the people who are looking at your account will be interested in.

If you want to sell an expensive watch, in order to sell that expensive watch to other people who are looking at your auction, they will need to feel comfortable. Two things come to mind, A, you offer good merchandise and B, that you really do know what you are doing when it comes to selling watches. They do not want to make a mistake on spending money on a watch that is worthless, they want to make sure that you know what you are doing and that you are offering good merchandise. So if the potential buyers see, before they bid on your auction, that you have run many auctions for the same item, they will say to them selves, "You know, this seller, since he is focusing on watches, and has a lot of experience selling watches and since he is sold a *lot* of watches, he (or she) really knows watches." What will also happen is the people who buy watches from you, if they are satisfied with their experience, they will post positive feedback regarding the transaction. Then with potential bidders who will go to your account, they will be able to click on your name, read the feedback about all of your other transactions and say, "This person sells really nice watches, he does a good job, and I'd like to buy a watch from him (or her) because I trust him (or her) based on the feedback he (or she) is been given and I know he (or she) has experience selling watches because of how many auctions he (or she) runs for watches." They might even look at all the other auctions you are running at that time, and if all the other auctions are also for watches, then they will be more certain that you do know what you are doing, that you specialize in watches, and that you are knowledgeable in that area.

In order to take advantage of all of this, you must specialize in one specific product line so that people will get used to you and will know this is what you sell and that you are familiar with the product. Not only that, but by specializing in that product you are showing people that you are their best source for obtaining this product at a very, very good price and obtaining a product of very high quality. Where would you rather buy a leather jacket, at a store that specializes in leather jackets or a store that specializes in odds and ends, in clothing? Of course, you would rather buy a leather jacket from a store that specializes in leather jackets because they are the experts in the field. By selling those leather jackets exclusively, they will be investigating which are the best leather jackets, at what price to offer them, who are the best manufacturers to obtain the jackets from, and what is the best leather available on the market. Nevertheless, a store that is only specializing in odds and ends, they really have not taken the time to investigate what the best products are. Therefore, if people just see that you just sell a wide array of products, with no specialization, they will just assume you are buying whatever you can get for cheap and trying to sell it for a profit. No, you want to be seen as somebody who exclusively deals with that item and who has spent a great deal of

time making sure he has obtained the best possible merchandise for his customers, and who are your customers? They are every single person on eBay who
have bought from you, who is considering buying from you, and who is following your auctions. In addition, if you develop a good following within that product line, you might actually attract a wholesale account. A wholesale account is
someone who sees that auction that you have with a particular item on eBay, who
contacts you, and who seeks to buy a larger quantity from you.

So, in order to be able to decide what to sell on eBay, you want to make sure
that you will be able to become an expert and you do not want to wait a long time
to do that because you will make a lot of mistakes along the way, losing valuable
time. Just select a product that you are an expert at, now. Believe me when I tell
you, everyone is an expert at something! It might not seem like a big deal to you,
what you know about, but there is someone out there who prizes the information
that you know. They would love to be able to benefit from what you have to give
them.

If you are a teacher and you know what the best school books to use for kids
who are struggling with a certain subject, then you could actually go ahead, buy
those books, and wholesale them on eBay. As you market the product, let people
know you are a teacher and that you are familiar with this product. If you are an
electrician, you will know the best parts that you will need for electrical appliances or for wiring, in homes. If you are a car mechanic, you will know what the
best car parts are, to use if a carburetor breaks down or if someone is having trouble with his or her air conditioner.

For instance, maybe you are a cook who enjoys cooking a delicious dinner for
the family. Or maybe you do not have any hobbies, except cooking for the family,
maybe putting together a fancy recipe, and getting people together you like.
Guess what? You could write up your personal recipes and auction them off on
eBay. There are thousands of people out there, if not millions, who love to cook
and who does not love to eat? Therefore, for every person who loves to eat, there
has to be somebody who is going to cook for those people. If you have developed
some really good recipes, and could constantly develop more recipes for people,
then you could auction off those recipes. You could even go ahead, buy the raw
ingredients, and auction them off on eBay. Of course, it would have to be according to the rules and you would have to look into laws and regulations that would
apply to you. You could even make things less complicated, if you are a person
who loves to cook, why not auction off the best pots that you use in your cooking
process? You would not auction off you personal pots, you would look at the pots
you use in the kitchen and contact the manufacturers or wholesalers of those

pots, forks or spoons. You would go ahead and buy their merchandise, describe it on eBay, tell people what you use your pots for, what foods work in each pot for its best use, how to prepare the pots and you can even include free recipes as a bonus—along with auctioning off those cooking utensils.

You and everybody else has an expert inside. Sometimes it is hard to see within yourself and realize what you have to offer to other people. Once you closely examine yourself, you will see that you have something—no matter what your level of experience, education or what you currently do, but you have something that could truly benefit somebody else. You know something, you have some stories that have been passed down, some collections, you have gone through some events; you have had some experience that other people find extremely valuable. If you are somebody who, maybe you love playing board games, then why not find the best board games out there and auction them off on eBay? As you see, there are many opportunities.

Now, maybe if you are someone with a more professional background or a more advanced degree, you could focus on that. I know of people who specialize in dealing with exotic relics, or people who deal with gems, such as diamonds, and they go ahead and buy the best possible diamonds they can find on the market for a very good price, that people outside of that business, or market, would not know. People like myself; I would never know where to get jewelry at or below the wholesale price. Gem people can, because they have been in the jewelry business usually for many years, they know exactly where to go, and how to circumvent the major wholesalers and they know how to buy that jewelry directly from the source. Then they auction it off on eBay and they are able to deliver jewelry at wholesale prices, saving people up to 90% off retail prices, in many situations. Moreover, the people who go ahead and bid on those auctions for the jewelry and win those items, those people are extremely happy and satisfied with what they received.

Therefore, no matter who you are, no matter what stage in life you are at, no matter what age, everyone has something to offer someone else. Everyone is familiar with one specific product, everyone has come to develop a hobby or everyone has something that they enjoy, whether it is travel, art, music, or movies. Everybody has developed a job or a business that they can use, that they can apply and make money from, on eBay. So whether you decide to focus on a religious area, social area or business area, make sure, and I cannot repeat this enough, make sure that it is something from the beginning that you know well, in and out, because guess what? People will definitely notice it whether you know what you are talking about or not. If you are not familiar with what you are auctioning off, people get discouraged very soon. If people who look at your auction description say to themselves, "This person really knows what he (or she) is talking about!" they will feel very encouraged to buy the item. Then they will think, "I am buying from an expert, I am buying from someone who has done their research, who will make sure to offer me what they are truly representing and will make sure to deliver something that I truly needed. How do I know that? Because obviously you are familiar with this area, you have investigated this area and used products or services in this area and now know exactly what I will need since I am also in this area and share similar interests." So make sure the product or service that you offer is a product or service that can clearly demonstrate to people that you are an expert in and you will be able to help them extract the best benefits of using your product or service. In addition, you will show them applications, that they on their own, may not have conceived before. If you can do that or if you can learn to do that, then I can show you great ways to start making money on eBay. Now with that, get ready for chapter three.

Chapter 3

Before you can start any business, you need to have the correct tools to start. Among the tools that an eBay business owner needs, are some tools found among all types of businesses. Such as a notebook, simple record keeping tools, a pen, a pencil, a ledger. You could use a software program to keep track of your business expenses, your revenues. You could use a good program to keep track of your customers. What's more important is that you also need to have a system that will allow you to stay organized. Being organized on eBay is extremely important, because at all times you are going to be buying many different products and you are going to be selling many things. You want to make sure that you are keeping track of the sources where you buy merchandise from, and the people who you are selling to.

You want to keep track of your auctions in progress and when you complete the sales, because if you do not stay on top of the buyers of your auctions, it is going to be hard to ensure that you always collect your payment. Not because people are looking *not* to pay you, but think about it, everybody has a very busy life and even if someone won your auction and intends to pay for the item they won from you, and they are very excited about buying it, they still might forget to buy it. You know, they are going to be busy with their own life and unless you remind them—which eBay gives you tools to remind them to pay for the auction—they might forget. So you want to make sure that you are very organized and that you have a system set up to always contact people who have won your auction.

You also want to have a system that allows you to keep track of leads. By leads, I mean people who respond to your auctions. For instance, you put up an auction for a box of comic books and you had five or six people e-mail you with questions regarding your auction. Therefore, you want to have a record of all the e-mail addresses of those people and if you can, you want to get their contact information so in the future you could always contact them when you have an auction for them. If you do not do this, what will happen is, you will have to rely on your actual auctions to generate revenue. Instead, if you are able to keep track of all the people every time you run an auction, when you get new merchandise, you will be able to send an e-mail or call up all the people who sent you inquiries, responding to them.

So for instance, where you put up an auction for a box of comic books, you received five or six people who sent an inquiry regarding those comic books. You could go ahead and you could send, the next time you have—perhaps you have bought, for instance—ten boxes of comic books from a comic book collector and this person has been collecting these books since the 1960s, and you know that the comics you bought are going to appeal to all types of comic book collectors. So you look back on your records and see, every time you ran an auction you received an average of five or six inquiries from different people. Now, if you have run five or six auctions in the past for comic books, at this point you might have thirty different inquiries from people, and you send an e-mail to each of those thirty people letting them know that you just bought a collection of ten comic books.

You let them know that you are willing to sell them one box of comic books for a certain price and if they are willing to take all ten boxes, you will sell them for a much cheaper price. You could even take this a step further and what you can do is, the people who contacted you, when they contacted you, I am sure that they were asking for specific types of comic books, and based on their questions you will be able to tell what type of comic books they are looking for. What you could also do is, you could e-mail people, and I strongly recommend that when you e-mail people, or however you contact them whether it is calling them on the phone, meeting them in person or sending them those e-mails, you want to find out from them exactly what type of comic books they are looking for.

Whether you are selling them comic books, baseball cards, clothing, or you could even be auctioning off cars, you always want to know the leads that you have. The people who have sent you inquiries regarding the products you are auctioning, you want to know what it is exactly that they are interested in and what it is that they are looking for. What I mean by that is, on one hand what it is that they are interested in, so you know when you have merchandise, right away you show them what you have. On the other hand, you also want to know within the genre that they are looking for, exactly what they want. For instance, if someone is looking for a used car, you want to know if they are looking at it for business or residential purposes. If someone is looking for old records, you want to know if they looking for classical music, rock music, pop music, country music and then even within those groups you want to develop as many subcategories as you can. When you receive merchandise, you can immediately contact those people and you might not even have to auction the item off on eBay because you might find a buyer much quicker and then you will not have to pay the listing fees and you will not have to give eBay a percentage of the sale. As you will see later on, eBay charges you two ways: one, when you list the item and you put it up for sale there is a charge and two, they charge you when you actually sell the item, keeping a small percentage of what the final price is. They will keep track on your account of how much you owe them and then you can pay by credit card or by check.

Now back to the topic about keeping track of your leads, which will of course take us back to the tools that you need for your eBay business. Keeping track of your leads is very important because these are the people who are going to be your customers and the lifeblood of any business is the customer. You will want a program that allows you to keep track of all your leads in two different ways. First, you will want to have people who just send you e-mails and second, you will want a list of people who actually purchased from you. The people that have purchased form you, if they are happy with your product, this is the reason why it is extremely important to always keep your customers happy. They are going to be the ones wanting to buy from you and they are going to be the ones *comfortable* buying from you because they have already done business with you.

The people who have sent you inquiries, they are going to be a little harder to sell because the only exposure they have had of you is seeing your auction or an advertisement or maybe hearing from someone else about an auction that you ran. Now, what do I recommend? I recommend two things. First, I recommend you have notebooks with you and keep a separate notebook for every category of merchandise that you auction off. Have a notebook for comic book sales, a notebook for baseball card sales, have a notebook for records, and have a notebook for clothing, or for whatever product you specialize in, or the products you will choose later on to specialize in. You want to make sure that you are organized and in order to very clear-headed, I recommend you have different notebooks.

Second, aside from having those notebooks you should also keep your records on a computer. Now, you might wonder about just keeping all those records on a computer. The reason is because on a computer, the only time you will have access to those records is when you are by your computer or if you go to another computer, you take a disk with you. That is not always practical. Sometimes you will be doing business somewhere else, and you will want to have an easy way to look up your customer base, and that is why if you have that notebook—the one you carry around, it will be very easy to look up your customers. Why is it also important to have a list of all the customers who bought from you on eBay and all the sales leads that you have through eBay?

Let us say you go to an auction, you go to a going out of business sale, or you meet with someone, a wholesaler or liquidator who is offering you a special deal on merchandise. You have never actually sold that type of merchandise before or maybe you have sold that type of merchandise, but you want to make sure that there is still a demand for that merchandise. So what do you do before you buy the merchandise? You open up your notebook, you look through your customer list, you look through the people who have inquired about your auctions, you call them, and you say to them, "Is this the type of merchandise you are interested in? Is this the type of item, that if I put up for auction or if I sold you directly, you would be interested in buying?"

Now, what can you also do at the time, since this could be merchandise that you are not familiar with and do not know what the going rate for this merchandise is, you could ask your customers at what price they would be willing to buy this merchandise at. If they for example, say they are willing to pay for old, quartz watches for ten dollars a piece. Then you know that since you want to keep for yourself, at least a 50 % profit margin, and you want to be able to double your money, the most you would pay the wholesaler or liquidator for those watches is five dollars. The same can be applied any time you find merchandise. Whether it is going to a garage or whether it is going to an estate sale, you want to have a list of people you can call right away to find out if the merchandise you are looking at is worth purchasing. In order to do this, you do not have to always have your customer base, and why do I say that? Because, after awhile you will become familiar with what it is that people buy and at what prices they buy it for. Therefore, you will be able to make your decisions without having to consult your customers every time.

You know another reason why it is very important to keep your customer base? Because an eBay business is similar to any other business, in the respect that the customer base is an asset and if you have a list of customers you will be able to sell that asset base to someone, one day, because you *might* want to sell your eBay business, one day. I have seen sellers on eBay, selling their businesses and they have done very well. There was one seller, I believe, that got around $12,000 dollars for his eBay business. Now that is not small change! Especially since after he sells his business, he sells his customer list also and he can move on and do other businesses, and if there is not a competition agreement; he can start his own business. You need to have a method for keeping track of all your customers, all the inquiries, and you also want to have a list, the same way you are keeping track of your customers, of all the people you can buy merchandise from. This way, when you run out of merchandise, you can contact these people and ensure that you can always have a substantial amount of merchandise available for your customers.

Another thing you need yet do not even need to have at home, is a computer. Especially if you are going to start working from your house, you will want to be able to save costs at the beginning. One of the biggest costs associated with an eBay business is a computer, right? You want to have a computer to keep track of your sales on eBay, to be able to look at your sales, and you want to be able to respond to e-mails. Now, if you are very short on funds or you simply just do not want to spend a lot of money with your new eBay business until you see how the business goes and to see if you will make money or not, you still want to always keep track of your expenses and minimize your expenses, when possible. Therefore, if you are just starting out with your business and you are only auctioning off a few items at a time, you do not need to have a computer at home. What you can do is use a tape; you could go to the office, or to a library and when you go to the library, you could use their computer, actually anywhere where there is a public computer. If you currently have a job and your employer allows it, you could spend a few minutes using your office computer to run your eBay business. Especially if at the beginning you are just going to have a few items up for auction, then it is not going to take much time. Buying a computer for $1,000 or $2,000 is a big expense, especially in these times. Now, remember—with an eBay business you should always consult with a professional about this, a lawyer or an accountant, because an eBay business, like any business, lets you deduct your expenses off your taxes. That computer should be a tax-deductible expense.

At some point, you do want to have a computer. Whether it is at your home office or your work office. That way you can always keep track of your auctions and as the volume of your business increases, you will be able to rapidly respond to people's e-mails, and be able to check your auctions. One thing that happens, is, when you are getting near the end of the auction, you will always want to be right by the computer to ensure that if there are any inquiries you answer them right away and if there is any other information you need to post in your auctions, then you can do it immediately. Moreover, you will not be able to have use of a computer if you are depending on a public computer at a library. You always want to ensure that you have access to a computer, whether it is having a computer in your work or your home or wherever your office might be. Second, you will want to have a good connection to the internet. Having good access to the internet is essential because eBay is an online market place and many of the communications you will be doing with your customers is through e-mail. So in order to be following them, you need to make sure that you always log-on. Now, if your funds allow and it is available in your area, I recommend that you get a DSL connection or you get a cable modem connection. Both of those connections will allow you very quick internet access, and also allow you to upload your pictures very quickly, let you navigate through eBay with ease and speed, which is essential to be running this business in a serious fashion.

Mentioning pictures takes us to the next tool that you need for an eBay business. You need to have a digital camera. A digital camera will allow you to take pictures of the merchandise and instantly download those pictures onto your computer. I even recommend a digital camera over a scanner. You see, a scanner allows you to put something on the scanner and the scanner makes a color photocopy, but it does not really allow you to take a picture, especially when you need to see 3-D qualities of an item. A digital camera, like any other camera, allows you to take a good picture of the item you have for sale and also allows you to take pictures from multiple angles and put all those pictures on your auction description.

Now, when you think about a digital camera, I am sure that you realize there are many types of digital cameras. First, there are pixel levels; the pixel level will be the quality of the actual picture: how many dots, what the resolution is, it will also take into account the defined quality of the picture. Therefore, you want to have a digital camera with at least a pixel level of three. You could get a pixel one, or two, even go all the way up to five. Number 3 should be sufficient, but of course, the higher you go from there, the clearer your picture will be. There have been studies done on eBay that the better the quality the picture is, the more people are attracted to the auction, and hopefully the higher the bids will become. It is essential to have pictures up at all times in your auction. Even if it is an item that people are intimately familiar with, such as a VCR or a television, people still like to see what it is that they are bidding on before they actually go ahead and place their bid. So make sure that you get yourself a good digital camera. Most digital cameras come with a UBS connection wire that connects your digital camera to your computer, which lets you download the pictures. Once you have the pictures up, you want to make sure that you have software that is usually included with the purchase of the digital camera. You want software that allows you to edit the pictures because you will want to crop the pictures. Cropping the pictures means cutting out anything from the picture that is not essential besides the actual item. In this way, you will be able to cut out the background. If you take your picture, let us say, on your desk, and on the desk was a book or notebook or a picture or maybe there was something in the background that you just want to eliminate, you want to be able to use software to edit the picture and get rid of it.

Now, once you have a good digital camera, the next step is to make sure you have an area where you can always work. You want to have an area that is organized, where you can store the merchandise. You will want to have one area of the storage for the merchandise that is waiting to be sold, meaning items that are waiting to be taken pictures of, items you have not processed yet. You will want to have the area where you have everything set aside. Then you will have another area that is actually your working area, where you take pictures of the items, you sit down, you write a good description of the item while you are looking at it, this way it is fresh in your mind and you can think of the attributes that will make that item exciting for people.

Next, you take one area within your storage area, or wherever you might work, and you put the items that have already been listed up on eBay for sale and you have those items ready to be shipped. You want to have another area where you actually do the packing for your items. Once someone has bid on those items, they have purchased it and sent you the payment, you have received it, and now you are ready to send the items out. You will want to have a good area that is clean. An area where you can package your items, have your boxes ready, store your packing supplies and also have a corner where you can put the items that UPS is going to come pick up, if you decide to send through UPS, or whether you are taking the items to the post office. This way everything is organized.

You see, one of the downfalls of many people who run eBay businesses is—and I will have to admit at the beginning of my own eBay business I had many challenges associated with this—is that once people send you the payment, you want to be able to send out their merchandise in a very efficient manor. This way, everything is shipped and your customers get the merchandise they purchased from you in a timely manner. One of the things I had a challenge with, was as my business grew, I was getting so disorganized, I had so much merchandise around that it was hard to keep track of what needed to be sent out, when and to whom. I developed a system that allowed me to be organized and I strongly recommend that from the beginning, before your business spirals out of control, that you do have an organization setup—you basically have a chart where the items will be corresponding to what stage of the process those items are on. Those are the items you will need.

You will want to have a phone; you will want to have a number where people can call you up. I always list my phone number on all of my auctions. This way if people decide not to call me, if they want to e-mail me or maybe if they do not even want to e-mail me at all, maybe all of their questions are answered in the auction description. By giving people my phone number; I am letting them know that I am accessible to them and if they have any questions they can contact me. They do not have to be worried that after they send their payment that I will simply disappear and they will have no way to contact me. This way I give them my phone number and sometimes people feel more comfortable speaking to a person before they place their bid just to make sure they know who they are dealing with. People call me up, especially during the last two hours of the auction. They will call and then ask any questions that they have. That is what I recommend; that you always have a phone number so that people can reach you.

If you are operating your business from home, at some point I recommend, when it becomes affordable, a separate phone line for your business. Otherwise, it will not sound too professional if a customer calls you up and one of your kids answers the phone. Or maybe one day you are tired and forgot that you listed this phone number as your business phone number and you pick up the phone and you might not be in the best of moods and the next thing you know, you blow a sale away. You always want to be in a situation where you have the ability to communicate efficiently. Customers, especially by being able to let them call you, being able to get on the internet quickly, being able to answer their e-mails, appreciate those kinds of communications. You might also want to have a fax machine. Sometimes, although it happens rarely, you will want to be able to fax a more lengthy description of the item you have for sale. Maybe you have met a supplier who wants to offer you merchandise, you will also want to allow him or her to send a fax of what merchandise they have available. That concludes this chapter. I hope this chapter was helpful to you and now you will move on to the next chapter, which is learning how to locate the merchandise you have decided to buy and sell.

Chapter 4

Now, in this chapter I am going to discuss one of the most essential aspects to your eBay business. This aspect is the ability for you to find the best locations to get your merchandise. By that, I mean I am going to discuss methods for acquiring a steady source and supply of merchandise; because it is not enough to just have a good source of merchandise. You need to make sure that source is steady, whether it is one source or a combination of sources. You want to able to have a constant flow of merchandise coming in so you have what you need to sell on your eBay business, especially, if at any time your source of merchandise is disrupted. You do not have the ability to put up new merchandise for sale, because two things will happen. One, you will disrupt the flow of making money; as your revenues will be halted until you have more merchandise to sell. Secondly, you might lose a lot of your customers and potential customers to your competition, because you will not have more merchandise to sell. You always want to be able to ensure that your sources of merchandise are good, solid sources. Now, many sources that I am going to discuss are going to be sources that are not steady by nature. Of course, by their nature because of the type of source that they are, they are going to be rare and will only become available once in awhile. Those sources are still good sources as long as you do not rely on them exclusively. Meaning, you are going to learn to locate those sources, but you will always keep in mind that underneath those sources, you will have to have your regular venues for obtaining merchandise.

Ok, so let us start out by selecting one category. Now, your category might be different because you could select to sell something else on eBay, but you are going to select one category, that is a general category—which no matter what, no matter what it is you are selling, you will be able to apply what you're going to do, with this category. You can apply this to your own category. So say your category is about books, new books. Books are an item that always seems to be in demand and I am sure there will always be a demand for them in the future. It is an interesting item because there are always new books coming to the market. There always a wide plethora of books available, there are different genres, there are different categories, there are soft-covered books, and there are hard-covered books; so there are many types of books you could choose from. Books, like many products, are easy to find because there are specific manufacturers (publishers), who produce the books and there are wholesalers who put out those books. There are also distributors who help get the books to the stores, and then the retailers who carry the books. There are many ways you could find books. You could start from scratch; you could actually just walk into a bookstore, wait until they have a good sale on books, go into their discounted rack, buy those books and put them up for sale. Now, you are not going to have a very wide profit margin if you do it that way, but you *will* be able to find books.

The next step is, you contact the wholesaler and find out from them what the minimum purchase you have to make is, then you set up a wholesale account, and you buy books from a wholesaler. You make sure to develop a good relationship with that wholesaler, as a good relationship is essential. This way that wholesaler will remember you when they have a special inventory or a special price on the inventory and they will call you up and offer it to you. If you become a good customer of theirs, the wholesaler will keep you mind when they themselves receive a good supply of merchandise from the publishers or their own sources.

Now, you can also use what is called closeout brokers. A closeout broker is somebody who is always on the lookout for merchandise based on a request that has been given to them. So, if you are looking for nonfiction books, dealing with cooking, you can call a closeout broker and say to them, "I am looking for a thousand hardcover or soft-cover books, dealing with cooking. The most I can pay for these books are a dollar apiece including shipping, or maybe a dollar twenty-five, including shipping. I need these books by this date and the books must be in this condition." The closeout broker will then go ahead and contact all of their sources, and their contacts and look for that merchandise for you. I would label a closeout broker as somebody who is not a steady source because a closeout broker, while he or she will work very hard to find the merchandise for you, might come up dry and not be able to find the merchandise you need. This is still a good source to always have, this way, when they are able to obtain merchandise at a special, discounted rate you could jump on that opportunity and buy that merchandise.

So you have a wholesaler who you can always rely on for a steady source of merchandise, probably at a 50 % discount to the retail price, and you have a closeout broker who might find you merchandise at up to 50 % off the regular wholesale price which would be great savings! Another source you should consider are auctions. Auctions are great because at auctions even if it's great merchandise, the auctioneer might not have attracted the right bidders for their auction. I have gone to many auctions where I saw great merchandise going for next to nothing. Sometimes the merchandise went for pennies on the dollar. One time, at an auction, I saw small bottles of champagne that retailed for $4.99 a piece, sold at the auction for twenty-five cents a piece. There is plenty of room to make money. At auctions, as long as you know what you are doing and you make sure that the merchandise you are buying is in good condition, when you sell it, the people who buy the merchandise from you, your customers, will be happy with it. Auctions are also great sources for merchandise because when you can go to an auction, first, you never know what you will find, and if you do find the merchandise that you are looking for, by the nature of an auction and as long as you are careful with what you bid, you could pay a very low price. Also at auctions, you are setting the price, because you are deciding the most you are willing to bid for that item.

Another source is garage sales. When you go to a garage sale, you will usually be dealing with used merchandise, but in many instances, you will find merchandise that is new simply because the person having the garage sale could have received that merchandise as a gift and he or she does not have a use for that merchandise, so they sell it. At a garage sale, it is very customary to find books among other items for literally twenty-five cents apiece. If you could buy items for twenty-five cents apiece and resell them for three, four five or twenty dollars apiece, you will have a lot of room to make money. Think about going to a garage sale and finding art. You could find paintings for a dollar apiece, turn around, and sell those paintings on eBay for up to three, four-hundred dollars. As you can see, garage sales are *also* a great source.

Now an estate sale is similar to a garage sale in the sense that the merchandise that is being sold belonged to a consumer, to a private individual as opposed to a business, and now that individual does not have use for that merchandise and the merchandise is being sold at a very cheap price. Now the difference between an estate sale and a garage sale is that an estate sale is run by a professional. It is similar to an auction in the respect that there is an auctioneer running it, except they are not an auctioneer, but this person who is running the estate sale is in business to conduct estate sales. So usually what the person running the estate sale will do is, they will investigate what the retail price of that item is and say to themselves, "What will most people be willing to pay for this price?" And they will look to sell it at that price. You see, at a garage sale you could get merchandise a lot cheaper because the person who is doing the sale, he or she has not investigated the value of the item and he or she probably does not even care what the item is actually worth. They are just looking to raise some cash. Maybe they want some extra money to go on vacation and maybe they figure they will just throw out the merchandise, anyway.

At an estate sale, the person is investigating the merchandise that they have for sale because their intention is that they want to make money and not just for the person they are conducting the estate sale on behalf of, they also want to make money for themselves. Either, they have purchased the entire estate and now they are selling or they have actually gone ahead and made an arrangement where they are getting a commission based on what their total sales are. So, of course, they will try to get as much as possible. Now, even though at an estate sale the people who are running the estate sales are more savvy and know the value of the merchandise, it is still great to go. In many instances the people running the estate sale were not able to determine the value of the item or maybe to them in their market, their local market, that item does not have much value, and the market you are selling to might give that item *more* value.

Let me give you an idea, with the example of books. You sell old Victorian books; you sell old English books from the early 1800s. Now, if somebody is conducting an estate sale in a small town in Oklahoma, in that town for instance, while people might love books, there might not be a specific market for English books from the 1800s. Since you have developed a business selling merchandise on eBay, you might know, first of all, if you will have a following for those books. There will be plenty of people coming to you looking to purchase those books from you and you might just know, by essence of your business, that as soon as you put up an item such as a book from the early 1800s from England, you will attract a lot of bidders for that item. The person running the estate sale has no way to reach those customers you could reach. Therefore, they will be willing to sell the book for a very cheap price. The same applies to many different types of items. And also, even if the person conducting that estate sale knows the value of that item, they are not a retailer who has the opportunity to sell that item, have that item sit on a shelf and let people look at their merchandise six or seven days a week, until the merchandise sells. The estate sale people only have that one day to sell the item. They know if they do not list that item at the estate sale for a very, very good price, they are not going to be able to sell their merchandise or to attract any interested buyers. Once an estate sale closes at five, six, or seven o'clock at night, it is over—the estate people do not have any more opportunity to make money with their merchandise.

Estate sales are great because when you go there, first of all, the merchandise at estate sales is generally nicer than at garage sales because the person running the estate sale will not conduct the sale unless he or she can make money. The only way for him or her to make money is if there is merchandise there that people will be willing to buy. Hopefully their merchandise is more expensive and worth more in value, so they can make more money. Therefore, when you go to that estate sale, you can usually count on finding higher caliber merchandise then if you simply go to a garage sale. Now when you go to a garage sale on the other hand, the merchandise is very, very cheap and it is a lot cheaper then at an estate sale. So there are pros and cons to each one. Either way, whether you go to a garage sale or to an estate sale, keep in mind that as the buyer, you have the ability and the right to negotiate the price. You can always bargain—and bargaining is important because as a businessperson your profit margin is the difference between what you are selling the merchandise for and what you are buying it at. Unless you have a wide enough margin, you are not going to make a lot of money. You go to the estate sale, even if the person running the estate sale portrays the estate sale as a type of sale where there are no bargains because they want to make it seem very upscale or they might want to make it seem that the prices are written in stone. I am telling you from someone who has experience—going to both estate sales and garage sales—that prices are always negotiable and the pressure to sell is on the person conducting the estate sale because not all of the money that comes in from the sale belongs to them, only a certain percentage.

With a garage sale, you also have bargaining power, because the person conducting the garage sale, once again, *what are the items at the garage sale?* He or she does not want to keep them, so as long as you offer them a reasonable price, even if it is a very cheap price, most likely, they will take it. I have gone to garage sales where I have gotten merchandise for less then I even planned to buy it for. What happened is, I inquired of the person running the sale, how much the item was, and then the person, thinking they were going to have a hard time selling it, or maybe wanted to encourage me to purchase the item, offered me a very good price. I went to a garage sale in New Jersey and I found an antique model boat. Well, it might not have been so antique; it was from the early 1960s. So I do not want to make any of you readers who were born then feel like I am calling you old, yet as I am sure you are aware, to many collectors a boat from the 1960s, especially a nice model boat, is worth something. It looked like a big pirate ship and every piece was crafted to perfection. That boat had a lot of value. Now, I went ahead and asked that person at the garage sale how much they wanted for an item, and they said they wanted five dollars and I said, "Okay, let me think about it." I really was not that interested in the item, but you know what? I was thinking about buying it and when I decided to buy it, at that point, it was already twenty minutes later and I wanted to make sure that I remembered the price so I asked the person, "How much is the boat?" The person misunderstood my question and thought I was negotiating, that I was not interested in the prior price, so the person dropped the price to a dollar and a half! I ended purchasing that boat for a dollar and a half and you would be surprised to know that the boat has a value of over $150.

As you can tell, there are many opportunities to make money. If you spend your Sundays going to garage sales and every Sunday you find an average of ten items, which in turn gives you a twenty to thirty dollars profit per item, you are talking an extra $200-$300 a week in your pocket. Now, a garage sale, I would not consider a garage sale or an estate sale a steady source of merchandise because you will never know what you will find and there could be rainy weekends and people will not conduct estate sales or garage sales because they know people will not come out. Now, garage or estate sales are a good source of merchandise if it is accumulative. If it is some extra on the side, that you will not rely on. Perhaps you have a good relationship with a wholesaler, because you are purchasing your merchandise from a wholesaler or, as I will discuss soon, from a manufacturer or an importer. You have them as a good source of merchandise and then besides those, you have additional sources of merchandise such as garage sales, estate sales, auctions, going-out-of-business sales, liquidations, maybe special sales where a store wants to get rid of a certain type of merchandise.

Now, as far as I mentioned importers—importers are great because what they do is they bring merchandise, at very cheap prices from overseas, where the manufacturing costs for those items are very low. Those importers are in the business of working on volume, so if you can purchase in volume, you will be able to save a lot compared to the wholesale price, as compared to when you buy the same or similar merchandise from a wholesaler who is obtaining the merchandise from a factory here in the United States. Manufacturers work similar to wholesalers. Manufacturers are in the business of selling to wholesalers. The reason they sell to wholesalers as opposed to directly to retailers is that they know the wholesalers can take a larger volume from them and that there will be less hassle then having to locate many small retailers who only take a small stock at a time. You can either tell the manufacturer that you will now, at the present, purchase a large volume of merchandise, or that as your business grows, you will be purchasing a lot more merchandise from them. In that way, you might be able to set up a good relationship with that manufacturer.

You have many opportunities to find good sources of merchandise. If you make a list of them now, you have covered: manufacturers, wholesalers, liquidators, auctioneers, garage sales, estate sales, even retail stores where they might want to liquidate some of their merchandise. I actually heard of one couple who makes over $150,000 a year on eBay; their gross is around $250,000 and their whole eBay business consists of selling used C.D.s. By used C.D.s, I am referring to music C.D.s such as Guns N' Roses, U2, The Police, various country C.D.s, classical music C.D.s, even Spanish C.D.s. They go to used music C.D. stores and they ask the owners of the C.D. stores that if they have any C.D.s that are selling slowly; because they are willing to buy those C.D.s for one dollar each. They buy those C.D.s for one dollar each and then they resell them at an average of two or three dollars for a C.D. Of course they have their expenses, they have their shipping expenses, employees, who work out of their own house packaging C.D.s, mailing out those C.D.s, writing up the description of those C.D.s, but this couple is simply getting their merchandise by going to *used C.D. stores.*

There are many options for getting your merchandise. You could even produce your own merchandise. If you are a manufacturer, you could sell your merchandise on eBay. On the other hand, if you are a painter or an artisan or maybe you know great recipes, or you are a good writer and you write your own book, or maybe you can create paintings or drawings. You could put all that merchandise up for sale on eBay and this way your cost is diminished because the only cost involved is what was entailed to producing the merchandise that you, yourself, have made. There are many ways to obtain merchandise for your business and to conclude, make sure that whatever merchandise you are selling, you always will have easy access in obtaining that merchandise.

Before you move on from this chapter, I want to remind you of another method of obtaining merchandise. You can actually set up a relationship with a store, where you go ahead and you help that store sell their merchandise. The way you do this is, you contact a store in your area and tell them you will help them sell their slow-moving merchandise on a commission basis. For instance, you contact ten different stores that sells paintings, for this example, and you tell those ten stores, "Hey look, let me sell all those paintings you have that you are not able to sell. I will list them on eBay, take pictures of them, answer the inquiries, take the sales calls that are produced from the ad and do all of the dirty work. I will pack up the paintings, as well." Then you split the proceeds either 50/50, 60/40; however you decide to do it.

There are many ways to find merchandise and developing joint ventures is very good. You could develop joint ventures with manufacturers, wholesalers, distributors, liquidators, and auctioneers to help them sell their merchandise that, they themselves, are having a hard time selling, or they would just like to find a different outlet to sell the merchandise. It does not even have to be merchandise that they are having a hard time selling, it could be merchandise which sells very well and this would be giving them an additional outlet. Meaning, if they were able to sell through the current outlets that they have now, and if they were able to sell, say, a thousand units, through eBay you will be able to help them sell an additional two or three hundred units and, of course, you will have more revenue because you will be able to sell more merchandise. The best part for you is that you will never have to pay for that merchandise because you are selling it on a consignment basis!

In addition to that, you should have plenty of ideas come to mind. You should start thinking about different things that you could do in order to succeed with your business. Think about calling wholesalers who sell a product that you are familiar with and help them sell their merchandise and the best part—think about it—what a difference it would make to your business if you actually do not have to spend any money *purchasing* merchandise. You will never be in trouble if you cannot sell merchandise because you will not have any cost assertion with merchandise. It will not be as if you have sunk a lot of money into merchandise and have to recover the money from the inventory.

On the other hand, a retail business or even a wholesaler who purchased the inventory is in a much more challenging situation, because if they do not constantly sell their merchandise, they cannot afford to pay their overhead for their business. Which you, of course, will also have overhead, but it should not be a lot of cost like a wholesaler, a manufacturer or a retailer. Retailers also need to recover the money they have actually spent buying inventory. If you could avoid that cost, then you are way ahead of the game. You could spend money that otherwise, you would spend purchasing inventory, and instead, you could spend it on advertising and marketing costs. You could buy a great digital camera, a great computer; and you could also use it to purchase yourself a good internet connection. If there does come a time where there is a great closeout or liquidation on merchandise, since you have saved a lot of money by not having to purchase merchandise from these wholesalers, you could afford to spend that money to make a bulk purchase. For instance, I once found a great price on a trunk load of merchandise, it was actually children's socks and I was able to purchase that merchandise since I did not have money tied up in another inventory at the time.

If you set up these growing ventures with people, where you sell their merchandise with them and split the money with them, then you will not have to be concerned about tying up your money because you will have those funds ready when an opportunity presents itself or when you go ahead and make an opportunity for yourself.

Chapter 5

While you can make a lot of money when you build a substantial business on selling merchandise on eBay, you can also sell your services. By services, you can sell what you do on eBay and what do I mean by that? Every person has a special skill or talent which other people would be willing to pay for. For instance, a plumber that is good at fixing leaks or installing new pipes, his service is in demand of every homeowner who has a running leak or a runny faucet or is having problems with any pipes in their home or commercial building. An artist who loves painting as a hobby, their service is in demand from people who might want a portrait painting, or a painting of their house or just a painting to put up on the wall. There are many different types of services that people can provide. There are professional services, such as what an attorney could provide, or a doctor or accountant and there are other services, such as a handyman service. There are services for receiving counseling or business advice. You might have experience in setting up a business, so that you could help other people set up a their own business. You might have undertaken a large project remodeling a house or fixing your automobile; with your experience, you can supply that knowledge to other people who would be willing to pay for it.

eBay allows you to sell your services and how do you sell your service on eBay? First, when you write your auction description, you make it very clear in the title what service you are offering and in the description, you let people know two things. The first thing you let people know is what type of service it is that you are actually offering. Say that you are offering someone your consulting time, and through your consulting time, you are going to teach them how they can run their business on eBay. So the person who is actually reading the auction, initially they would have two questions. First questions they will want to know, is exactly what's included in your consulting; are you going to be helping them find merchandise, are you going to be helping them list merchandise, or are you going to help them decide what cameras they need to take digital pictures? Secondly, another important question that they are going to ask, is, what is your expertise; why should they pay you money in order to obtain knowledge, information, and help from you?

You need to be able to demonstrate that you are an expert. In order to demonstrate that you are an expert in your auction description, you have to list some of your qualifications; you will want to list some of your experiences, similarly to a resume. What you need to do, is, you need to be able to show people that the project you undertook or the job experience that you have is enough—and broad enough so that it could pass the topics and the areas that people are going to want to know from you. At the same time, you specialize enough so you will be able to help him with their detailed questions and able to offer them ways to grasp, especially with the finer points. Therefore, when you do offer your service to people and are paid for your service, they can see the value of what you are offering and recognize you as an expert.

Now, some other ways that you can be recognized as an expert is by listing your educational experience, whether it is undergraduate experience, an advanced degree or whether you went to graduate school and acquired an MBA, or other awards you might have received in the field, including any qualifications or special licenses you might have. Perhaps you are offering people advice on a personal project, such as remodeling a home, fixing the engine of your car, or advice on how to paint the interior of your home, or maybe advice on how to organize a wedding or family occasion. You need to show people very concrete samples of what you did. I would include pictures in the auction description of the actual project that you worked on. What you could also do is give people references of people who you dealt with through the completion of your project. When you undertook this project, whether it is actually your day-to-day work, your business, a sideline business, a part-time business, or whether it is a hobby that you have, you want to offer names and numbers of other people that were involved in the business or hobby with you. That way, they can contact as many as they feel they need to, or even if they do not contact anyone for questions, they will feel assured when they know that there are other people involved and that there are other people who you have dealt with.

Usually, if someone is going to pretend they are an expert in the field, they are not going to go as far as to list the people who they have dealt with because they will be afraid that someone will actually investigate, look into it and find out that they have made up what they are portraying to be true. Whenever people see that you are presenting such information as your degrees, your type of business or hobbies that you are involved with, or concrete examples of what you have done, that lends credibility to your auction. Especially if you can list dates, periods of time when you worked on the project, give names of people who were your suppliers, vendors, customers you sold to or people you bought from, or associates who were involved in the project with you. What you will also want to do, is to list a phone number in your auction so people can call you up.

Now I want to warn you about people calling you up. While you are going to be very excited that they are calling you and you are going to want to sell to them, you are going to want to convince them that they should bid on your auction and use your service, and you might be tempted into overselling. By overselling, I mean that you might end up, in order to prove the value of your auction and/or the service that you are selling, you might end up giving them too much information. You might actually go ahead and supply them with the advice that you are trying to auction off. Imagine that you are auctioning off an hour of consulting on how to write a book. When people call you on the phone, if in order to convince them to bid on your auction, you end up sharing with them your tips for writing a book in a very efficient and quick manor, then you will have nothing else to offer these people because they will have already received their information. Even though you have more information to offer, they will feel that they have everything they need to know, and they are not going to bid on your auction, losing your potential business.

What can you say when people call you on the phone? You can give them general ideas. Perhaps you are very good at writing very quickly. One of your tips for writing is not to look at the computer screen while you type. Instead of telling people that advice, even though you might have another hundred tips, you do not want them to feel that you have given away the most lucrative part of your advice. You can tell them, "I have developed strategies to write in a very quick manor without having to resort to being engrossed in the actual writing as you are doing it." Now, when you say something like that, you are being vague, and you have not given them any information that they can use as soon as they get off the phone with you, and at the same time you have given them an idea of the direction your consulting advise is going. In addition, what you should do when people call you up, is to be careful about giving out your sources. If you are giving someone consulting advice on how to start a business or where to obtain merchandise, do not tell them where you obtain your merchandise and do not be specific—let me do their own research and find the sources of your merchandise, themselves. You can tell them that you are an expert at locating distressed inventory, which the sellers no longer need; therefore, you are able to get it at a very cheap price. So instead of actually telling people that you get your own merchandise from liquidators or from business that are going out of business, you have given them an idea on what kind of merchandise you are going to find and have not connected them with your personal sources.

For example, an on-line entrepreneur had a few successful web sites where among the products that he sold were e-books. Now an e-book is a downloadable file, which contains the text of an entire book. People who visit the web site and purchase the e-book can download information straight to their computer. This individual, on his auction description, offered the highest bidder of his auction that he would spend a month with them on the phone, once a week, to speak for at least an hour and they could e-mail as much as they wanted, to each other. The person who would win his auction could send as many questions as they had and he would teach them everything that he knew about how to set up a web site to sell e-books. He would teach the highest bidder how to advertise and market it, what prices to charge, how to draw visitors to your site, and how to lend legitimacy to your site. So because he was very clear with what he was going to offer people and they *understood* what he was offering, people were able to see that he was an expert in the field. How did he do that? On the auction description, he listed the addresses of five of his web sites. Someone reading the auction description could go ahead, visit the web sites, and see that this person was conducting business the way that he claimed to be conducting business. Then if someone who visited his auction description was interested in selling e-books, then they would feel that this person is an authority in the field and is somebody who could teach them to sell ebooks, as well.

If you sent this individual an e-mail, while he would offer you general information, he never actually gave people advice that they could take and actually start using to make money selling e-books before they actually won the auction. He would state things such as, "I will show you how to sell e-books sufficiently." or "I will show you how to increase the sales of books you are currently doing now." or "I will show you how to pick a title for your book that outsells the current title that you have, for your e-books to sell." and "I will show you how to write an e-book." To give you some motivation to start offering your services on eBay, the auction won for over $500.

So this individual had no cost, except his time. The only time that he had to spend actively, the time he exclusively devoted to the project—the auction, was four hours a month he spent discussing with the individuals concerning their project, on the phone. The person who bought the auction, the highest bidder who won the auction, he had the right to call this individual at preset times, once a week for an hour. For four hours of talking on the phone, the seller received over $500. for his consulting advice and that comes out to $125. an hour. Unless you are making over $125. an hour, I think that is a very good reason to become excited. You would be surprised at how much money people are willing to offer for all types of information and advice. That does not mean it has to be a business—some people might want advice on how to get into a graduate school, how to get into a good college, or some people might want advice on how to pursue a certain type of career. Maybe someone needs career advice and if you have a lot of experience—maybe you are a head hunter or you worked in human resources at a company—then you could teach people how they can out find for themselves what kind of a job they want, or maybe you could teach them how to find the job that they want. Maybe you are someone who worked in a specific industry for a long time and you could help people succeed and excel in that industry.

For example, you are a banker and you have been working at banks for the last twenty-five years. You will have a lot of advice to offer as far as how you get a job at a banking sector, the best jobs in the banking sector, which jobs are going to offer the most promise and which areas will have the most growth in the near future and the long term future. You see, regardless of your background—you could be a college student, you could be a high school student, or you could be a senior citizen—there are many areas of interest that you have that match with other people's areas of interest. There is plenty of advice and plenty of life experiences, even if you are very young, that other people could benefit from.

So what I would suggest is that you spend some time, maybe now or tonight, sitting and writing down all of the different areas of information that you could be considered an expert on, or even make a list of things that you are knowledgeable about. It could be as mundane as playing a certain sport to having a passion for a certain language or being a connoisseur at a certain type of art. Whatever your area is of interest, whatever your areas of experience are, write them down. Then you could decide to auction off your experience to other people. You could list on an eBay auction, what your advice is, why it is that people will to want receive this advice from you, what makes you an expert in this area; and what it is that you are going to be offering people. Then you could go ahead and allow people to bid for the right to receive that information from you.

I think that as a side note, if you want to make any of your auctions successful, even when you are selling a physical item such as a computer or a painting, always include free advice and free consulting along with your auction. What I mean by that, is if you are auctioning off a brand-new computer, let people know in your auction description that you are going to be more then happy to talk with them through the process of setting up the computer. And if they have any questions they can e-mail you; you will be able to suggest different software, printers, and what are called peripheral devices they can use to get the most out of their computer experience. Even if you are offering a painting in your auction, you should give advice on the best way to frame the painting, what are the most quality frames, perhaps even suggestions on where to put the painting in the house.

See, any time you give someone free advice, it makes the person feel comfortable that you really are in it for more then just that one sale. It makes them realize that you really do want to help them, you care about them, you do not just look at them as a customer, you also look at them as a friend, someone you want to help and someone you want to make happy. You see, people are not used to a person of that nature, and merchandising in this age, where you have tremendous department stores the size of a football field, make people forget that everyone still needs personal communication and what people call a "personal touch." People want to know that there is someone on the other end who is going to be there to help them through the process. If you could offer people that personal touch in your auctions with your service or if you are auctioning off a physical product, people will be happy to do business with you as opposed to your competitors who do not go that extra mile to help them.

Chapter 6

One of the phenomena that exists on eBay is the intense competition. Similar to any other market, aside from what makes the competition fiercer in many instances on eBay, is that it is extremely easy for people to see your competition. Instead of people having to drive to the other side of town or walk a few blocks to find one of your competitors, on eBay, all they have to do is click on a mouse to look at complete listings of a certain product and they will be able to see every auction that mentions that product. So for instance, if you as a buyer are on eBay looking for basketballs, all you would have to do is type in the word "basketball" in the search and you could see all of the listings that come up with the word basketball. You could continue refining and narrowing down your search until you found what you wanted, and in almost all instances there will always be competition and other sellers offering the same product or services that you are offering.

One of the most important goals you want to accomplish on eBay is being able to stand out from your competitor. If you cannot stand out from your competition, you will be lost among all the other sellers because people are not going to have any reason to buy from you—and even if they do buy from you, they might not pay as much for your product or services, when they realize how many *other* people are selling the same product or service. On the other hand, if you can distinguish yourself from the other sellers who are selling the same or similar product, people will be willing to buy from you and they might even be willing to spend more money then they would have otherwise. Think about it, if you went to look for a very generic product at a store and that product was priced at your local super market at a much higher price than at another super market, you would probably go to that other super market if you had the time. Now, if it is a hard to find item, such as a new watch from a special company which is only producing watches in a very limited quantity, you would be willing to buy that watch, even if it costs more then other watches from less-known brands and which do not have the same reputation as this exclusive company. Therefore, what you want to do is apply that same strategy as an exclusive company with exclusive brands uses, when you market your own items on eBay.

The first thing you want to create for yourself is a brand name. To explain a brand name, you want a descriptive word where people know that you are a provider of quality merchandise or services on eBay. You want people to know that they can always find special offerings from you and when you do offer those special incentives, you give them free bonuses, as I mentioned before: the additional consulting, or you can give them extra items that supplement the merchandise that you are offering for auction. For instance, if you are offering a printer on eBay, you might want to include a ream of paper as a free bonus. This way, the person is excited because he or she knows when they receive this printer; they will also have paper, which they can readily use. Another way to distinguish yourself from the competition is by not offering any *single* items, instead, auctioning off bundles of related products. In the example of a computer printer, what you can do is to offer together with a box of paper, or together with a cartridge of black and color ink. You could also offer tips on how to best use the printer. So you see, you want to be able to distinguish yourself from the competition. You want to give people a reason to bid from you even though there are other people who are selling the same item.

Another way to make sure to distinguish yourself is to offer very good customer service; timely responses to any questions that people have, by answering e-mails promptly, and by giving as much project information as you have in the auction description. Another thing that is very important, even when people are selling the same item as you are—even when people are very familiar with the item already—is to include a few good pictures of the item. You would be surprised how many people prefer to bid on an auction, when that auction has very clear, colorful, and bright pictures of the item being offered, when there are other people selling the same item on other auctions. I have seen two auctions for the exact same item at the exact same time. The auction with the better description, more extensive description of the item, where the auctioneer provided more detailed information and had brighter and more colorful pictures; that particular auction attracted much higher bidders then the other auction. Since you make your money by obtaining a final high winning bid for your auction, you want to do whatever you can to encourage bidders to be drawn to your auction as opposed to another auction.

To summarize: you want to have an extensive description of your item where you want to give a lot of detailed information; you want to have very clear, bright pictures; and you want to offer free bonuses that are related to the product you are offering (you would not want to offer a record if you are auctioning a VCR and visa versa and you do not want to offer someone an extra movie if you are auctioning a record player). Another strategy is bundling your product and that can be done in many ways. If you are auctioning off a toy, you might want to find similar toys or ones that fit into that category and auction them together. When a parent looks for toys on eBay and that parent sees twenty different auctions going on for the same G.I. Joe figure, that parent—since they are probably buying that toy for their child or a grandchild, niece or nephew, needs to see something special that catches their eye. What you want to do is encourage that parent to purchase the toy from your auction. So how do you do that? If a parent is going to buy that present for someone, then they are looking forward to make the recipient of the present very happy. So the more that you can offer the parent—who will be giving this item on to someone else—that will encourage the parent to purchase from you, the better. If you can offer the parent a few toys in that auction, that parent might say to themselves, "Do you know what? I *do* need to buy toys for other children" or "I would love to be able to offer this child an even bigger present then I originally planed. I will go ahead and bid on this auction."

One thing that people always love is people who are attracted to collections. If you could offer them a collection of toys, books, baseball cards, or postcards, the fact that they are all received in a bundle—and that bundle is a collection—will excite them. They will know that they are receiving an assortment of products within a certain category that appeals to them whether it appeals to them because it is a present for someone else or whether they, themselves, want to enjoy it. Either way, they will be receiving a variety of items all related and they are also items that make that person happy. You could apply this principal even if you are offering what is not being collected or is not being given as a present. What do I mean by that? Let us look at auctioning off clothing.

Now clothing, I think you will agree with me, is the farthest thing from collectible toys or collectible baseball cards, so how can you take the idea of offering collections and applying it to clothing? Here's what you can do. If you are auctioning off used clothing or new clothing, you could assemble a group of clothing pieces that are complimentary to each other; you could put together a suit, two dress shirts, a belt, dress socks, three neckties and you could offer that as a ready-to-wear-wardrobe for the winning bidder. Now think about the person looking at your auction. When he is looking at auctions from all the other sellers, he will say to himself, "Look, I see that there are hundred different sellers offering suits at their auctions. I see another hundred sellers offering neck ties, and I see another hundred sellers offering belts, shoes, socks and fancy shirts and everything that someone could think of, for their wardrobe."

Then they see one seller offering in his or her auction an entire ready-to-wear-wardrobe. The person looking at that auction will become very excited because not only will they be able to instantly receive a complete wardrobe if they are a winning bidder, but also think about how much money and time they will save by not having to purchase those items through various auctions. Now, why would it be cheaper? Because, usually, the minimum bid is based on the item being offered. Now if someone is offering a dress shirt and the bidding starts at three dollars, the bidding may escalate to six or seven dollars before the auction is over. If that shirt is combined with a group of clothing, the next auction will probably also start at those minimum bids. Which would mean that the price would climb as bidders start bidding, and it would not become a cumulative effect, meaning, if someone were looking at five auctions for five different pieces of clothing, each of those auctions is starting at the minimum bid. Even if the auction only attracts four or five bidders to the auction, the price naturally starts building and then the winning bidders would have to purchase each one of those auctions separately. Compare it to the situation where you are bidding on an entire wardrobe: Even if the minimum bid is higher, where all of the bidders are focused on one auction— the final price on a per piece basis is lower.

Another reason a bidder would be attracted to an auction, whether it is an entire wardrobe or any other type of auction, is because being able to bid on only one auction and then hopefully buy that auction, will help to save a lot of money on the shipping. Think about how much shipping and handling would cost if you purchased from ten different auctions as opposed to only one auction. Since most shipping, whether it is done by UPS or the US Postal Service starts with a minimum price and then becomes cheaper incrementally only as the weight becomes heavier. What happens when you have to purchase from different sellers, is that the base shipping would be charged in each of those auctions. Especially if there is a handling fee, because as the weight increases it adds up with the shipping minimum being the same, and you still would have to pay the base shipping fee for each one of those auctions. That money taken out of your pocket is high.

On the other hand, if you purchase the auction, purchase one auction where you receive the entire wardrobe or an entire group of items, the base shipping is the same and you might actually receive a discount too, because if the total weight is substantial, UPS or the Postal Service could have a discounted rate. There are many advantages for the winning bidder to want to focus on the auctions with the entire wardrobe or an entire group of baseball cards or a group of books or a collection of comic books. The reason that you might be very interested in offering a group of items, as a seller, is because you might want to be able to charge less on the handling fee, which is a legitimate charge to cover your time preparing the auction and shipping it out. If you do not mind foregoing some of the handling fee, in order to sell this auction, you will attract more bidders interested in purchasing a group of item that are complementary to each other and the final bid might be a lot higher then if you split up the auction to five different lots.

Even though you are giving up the handling fee, that final bid, I believe, will compensate you for what you would not gain as far as handling charges go. If you look at my auctions, I never charge any handling fees and I would recommend you to do the same. You need to concentrate on making sure that the final bid, the higher bid, is substantially enough so that it compensates you both for your time and still gives you a decent profit from the auctions being auctioned off. Finally, what will also help you is by setting up this process, this auction, where people know that they could always obtain large lots or groups from you. People will look forward to seeing other groups of items you offer, because people love, especially in this day and age, *saving money*. They can make all of their purchases in one auction as opposed to splitting it up into five or six auctions. If they can buy everything from you at one time instead of having to go to local department stores to make all of their purchases, they will become very enthusiastic to buy from you and will keep your auctions on their list, tracking your auctions. It is good to remind them to focus on your auctions when you do have them.

However, the best factor is that you know you have a good reputation from these group items, these collections of items and the public will be inclined to bid on your auctions. That is a very good way distinguish yourself from other sellers, by always offering groups of items that are complementary to each other: By offering collections, free bonuses, quality service, free consulting, giving people advice, tips and strategies and how to get the best, efficient use out of either the service or the merchandise that you are offering. I would also recommend not charging handling fees in order to show people up front that there are not going to be any hidden costs and that you are only charging the actual cost of the shipping.

Chapter 7

Many sellers on and off eBay make one of the most lethal mistakes that can be made in business. This mistake, which can be disastrous in any business whether small or large, is competing based on price. By competing based on price I mean that is what many people do in business to differentiate themselves from competitors, in order to gain a larger share of the market. In order to be able to sell more, they start competing based on the price. What they do, I am sure you have seen many gas stations do, and many stores do, they keep lowering their price until they are cheaper then their competitor, which hardly ever lasts long because then the competitors will rush to match their prices. What these sellers will do, is they will always lower their prices to try to be the cheapest in the market. They hope that while their prices are lower for that period of time, they will do a lot of business—they will make money and they are looking to make money based on volume because they are foregoing many of their profits.

The reason this idea, this strategy is very misguided, is because you could never compete in price—there will always be somebody cheaper then you and there might always be somebody who is willing to take a loss in order to gain market share. For instance, if they bought an item for a dollar, and they have enough reserves in their bank account to weather a loss in their business for two or three months, they might actually sell that item that cost them a dollar, for only ninety-cents. The reason they do this is to drive their competitors out of business and then in the future they will be the only players in the market. They also do this to gain the reputation where the public knows they can buy items cheap from them. Once your customers get used to buying from your them, they could always raise the prices and hope that the customers will continue buying from them. The reason that this is always a big mistake and you should always avoid this is that, as mentioned, it is very hard to compete in price. Especially if you always offer your item at a very cheap price, people will start perceiving it as inferior quality or they will just decide that there is something wrong with that item and they are not going to want to buy from you. People want to know that sources of merchandise are good, steady sources. If they are going to buy from you, if they are going to commit themselves to a relationship where they are obtaining that item from you, they want to know that you are going to be there in the future.

If you offer an extremely low price, you might be inadvertently telling them that you are not going to be in business for very long. Maybe you are actually going out of business now, that is why you are blowing your inventory or maybe it is the reason you are offering your services for such a cheap price, and they will wonder if you are going to be there in the future. If your competitors are offering their prices at cheap, but more reasonable prices that makes sense at what the rest of the market place is charging, then your potential customers will decide to buy from another individual. They figure since this individual is offering a more reasonable price, they are more secure in the market. They are offering a better quality product and they are going to be around for the long term. What you will want to do is, always be able to distinguish your product, as I have mentioned in the past, in order to make sure that you are not forced into competing based on price. If you see that there are a lot of people selling the same product or if most of the market is used to buying a generic product, then you want to seek out a product within that category, that is either branded or carries a designer name. Names such as Nike, Tommy Hilfiger, Levi's, Calvin Klein are examples, or you might want to introduce a product with unique features that the products from the competitors do *not* have.

If you are introducing a VCR to the marketplace when other people are selling VCRs, you might want to sell a VCR with special features that are not available in other models. When you offer your VCR, you might want to include a booklet that will teach even the most inexperienced person when it comes to programming VCRs and I think that can be said for most of us. You might want to offer a booklet to the public that will allow anyone to program that VCR within five minutes. Even though the VCR you are offering is similar to the other VCRs, or it might even be the same VCR, when people see that you are offering this booklet that will teach you something that 95% of the people out there do not know how to do, they will be interested. Then they will be willing to buy from you and they might be willing to pay a little more because you are offering them a benefit that they need and is directly related to the VCR that they are purchasing from you.

Another way, as mentioned before, to distinguish yourself, is when you sell an item at a competitive price, you obtain an exclusive product from a manufacturer or distributor. For instance, if you know of a manufacturer or you can find a manufacturer that produces a very exclusive chocolate, you can contact this manufacturer and say that you would like to be their exclusive online distributor of chocolates. If they already have a web site, then you could offer to be their exclusive online eBay distributor of chocolate. Tell them that the reason it is worthwhile to them as a manufacturer or distributor to set up this exclusive arrangement with you, is that in having another venue sell their merchandise, you will become a good, long term customer who will be buying a lot from them as time goes on. You could also let them know that the more people that purchase their product, the more that their chocolate is exposed to, even greater brand recognition than their chocolate will have in the general marketplace. Meaning, the public buys the chocolate from you on eBay and he or she enjoys it, then the next time he or she walks into a retail store, they will ask for the same chocolate. That will help the chocolate vendors, because the stores will send inquiries to the manufacturer looking to set up a wholesale account, and to look into purchasing chocolate from them. You are offering this manufacturer of chocolate two benefits: One, the purchases you will be making directly to them in order to resell the chocolate on eBay, and two, you will also be offering them increased brand recognition in the marketplace.

Another example of an exclusive product is a shoe made in Italy, a style that is not widely available in the United States, or is not even available at all. You could contact different manufacturers overseas or you could contact importers and ask them to obtain for you a special product that might not be expensive, at all. The item might only retail for a dollar, but if the item is exclusive enough and if, for instance, is a novelty item, people might get excited and want to buy that item from you on eBay. Then you will not have to compete based on price, because you are the only one offering the novelty item.

There are many manufacturers, distributors, wholesalers and importers out there, who have exclusive relationships with a source of merchandise and they themselves, are acting as the middleman and are constantly looking for a marketplace through which they can sell their product. If you can set up an exclusive distributorship with them and have the exclusive right to sell on eBay, then you can be assured that you will not have any competition. What if you ask me, "If that same product is being sold in retail stores locally in my area, how would I still gain by having that product sold on eBay?" You would, because especially in rural communities, they might not have access to that product, or they might not have a store near them that carries that item. Secondly, even if there is a store near them that carries the exact same item you are offering them, the convenience of being able to purchase the item online and having it shipped directly to their home or office can be irresistible. Which raises an important point—whenever you conduct an auction, always make sure to offer people, or to ask them whether they want the item that they have purchased sent to their office or their home.

Among all the other items they offer exclusively on eBay, of course as long as it is conforming to the rules on eBay, would be artwork from an artist who might be well-known. They might not have the technological knowledge or might not be familiar with the internet and they might not be selling their artwork on eBay. You should contact this artist, form a good relationship with them, be upfront and honest, and offer weekly and monthly reports of the progress of the auctions in which you are selling their artwork. Then you could go ahead and list the paintings of this artist and since you will be the only source for this artist's paintings, artwork or sculptures online, you will have a marketplace that needs to buy from you if they want to purchase the artwork. Now, in order to make sure the artwork does sell, you need to do what was discussed in the earlier chapter and provide as much information as you can about the artist and the paintings being offered. You also want to have really sharp-looking pictures that will show people the beauty of the artwork being offered.

What else can you offer on an exclusive basis, in order for you to distinguish yourself from your competitors? You could contact toy manufacturers and ask them if they have any lines that have not been moving, lately. For instance, there is a toy manufacturer located in Arkansas and most of the toy manufacturers' lines are located in Arkansas. It just so happens that a certain horse and buggy toy model that they made had not been selling well. You ask that manufacturer for the exclusive right to sell that toy horse and buggy on eBay. The reason that manufacturer would be more then happy to give you that exclusive license to offer the item on eBay is because no one in the stores are buying it and suddenly they have another outlet to sell that item. Once you can demonstrate that you can sell their merchandise sufficiently and quickly, they might be inclined to give you exclusive rights to their other products. Now, you might ask, if an item is not selling well in Arkansas, then why would it sell on eBay? You see, Arkansas is a large state, they have a large population, and you would think that if no one wants a certain toy in that entire state, that there is no market for it, but you have to remember that same toy might be appealing to people who live in other states. With the example of the horse and buggy, that toy may be appealing to an adult who grew up on a farm. Now that person is living in New York or New Jersey or Washington D.C. and they might love to purchase the toy either as a collector's item for themselves or to give it to their children or grandchildren. You see, you have to remember that even if a certain product is not popular in a particular area, there could be a demand for it in other places.

What I would suggest is that you make yourself a list of manufacturers and you can do this by going online. First, decide what you want to offer on eBay, what kind of product you want to offer, and then look for manufacturers that produce that item. You could also contact wholesalers, distributors, or importers that work with the items that you want to sell. Contact them and let them know what it is that you want to do, how you plan on selling it, and do not bother worrying about people stealing your idea and selling it themselves on eBay because most people are not familiar with eBay and do not know the full potential that eBay has to offer. Therefore, even if you tell them you are going to sell the item on eBay, they might not be inclined to copy you because they most likely will not see the potential that exists on eBay. Once you have exclusive rights on eBay, make sure that you get it in writing, so if your sales start taking off, no one can take the exclusive deal away from you and start selling the item, themselves. Another reason why selling exclusive items distinguishes yourself from competitors is, A, you never have to compete based on price, and B, when you sell these exclusive items you will build a very good reputation for offering items that your competitors do not offer. You will have items that no one else in the marketplace offers and a following of people who look forward to seeing what other exclusive items you will be offering, in the future. So remember, never compete based on price, otherwise you will catch yourself in a cycle of never-ending competition. Now there *will be* times you will want to compete based on price or when you are forced to compete based on price. Those instances are usually when you are offering a generic product that is easily copied by anyone or one that is being offered by many people. In order to distinguish yourself, even though to some extent you will still have to compete based on price, is to use the tools and strategies that was mentioned before, to differentiate as much as possible from your nearest competitor.

Chapter 8

A stumbling block that many entrepreneurs come across when they are starting their business is determining what the true market value of their products and services are. When they are ready to sell their products or services, they do not know in many instances what the going market price is, if they are offering a unique product, or, if their product is differentiated from their competitors, they do not know the right price to charge. What I always recommend in those instances is to test a market. What eBay allows you to do, is to put up a single item or to advertise your service in a very limited basis. Of course you need to advertise as much information as possible and let the marketplace determine the correct price for that merchandise. What will then happen, is, as the auction progresses and the public sends you e-mails and calls you up and you contact people, you will see what the fair market value of the product or service is, that you are offering.

What you do not want to do is set a very high opening bid, by that I mean the lowest price that someone could bid on your item because then, if you have over-estimated the value of your service or product, people will not bid on the item and they will simply ignore your auction. On the other hand, if you are not excited enough, and you do not see the value of what you are offering, other people will not pick up on it, either, and they will not want to bid on your auction whether it is for a product or service. People want to see enthusiasm; they want to see the reason why they should be excited to purchase the product or service. If you believe in what it is that you are offering, your enthusiasm will be "contagious," and people will that what you want to offer them is something of value and most likely they will become excited, as well. What you can always do, if you see that you have an item that is not attracting any bids, you can always change the item you are offering. You can always modify the item, offer an item with different features or a service more geared toward the marketplace, but what you should *not* do—and I cannot stress this enough—is to get caught in a price competition game or undersell your product, lowering its value.

It is important to remember that the public's perception is very closely related to the price that the product is being sold at, especially when it comes to a service. People want to know that the service that you are offering and are receiving, is of professional value. That is why the some of the most successful lawyers are the lawyers who charge the most. You could say that they charge the most because they are so successful. However, I am willing to bet that there are many lawyers who are very successful, who are very intelligent, who know a lot about the field and have many years of practice yet they still do not make as much money as the lawyers who charge more, simply because the other lawyers are charging more. You see, both lawyers might have the same twenty clients who give them consistent work throughout the year, but the lawyer who has convinced their clients the value of their services are worth 20% more then the other lawyer, will simply make more money with the same amount of clients. Now, I am not asking you to double your price compared to what your nearest competitor charges, but what I am advising you to do is go ahead and to market and sell your products or services at the value that they are worth, or rather at the value that you feel they are worth. Be confident in yourself and other people will notice the confidence that you have. The most important part is knowing the true market value of the products and services that you are offering because you can now go ahead and contact potential buyers and let them know what you are offering and circumvent the entire auction process by allowing them to purchase your product or service directly from you.

This way, when you contact people who are in the market for what it is that you are offering, you will sound confident when you insist on the price that you are asking. People will always try to negotiate with you on the price that you are asking. They will always try to negotiate with you based on price, they might say, "You are charging too much," or, "I could get it cheaper somewhere else," or, "Your product or your service is not worth the money you are asking for." If you have already tested out the market on eBay, then you already know what the going market rate is for your product or service. Then you will have no problem letting those potential buyers know that since what you are offering is of high quality and people are happy with it and have been satisfied with their experience using your product or service that they, too, might enjoy using your product or service and they need to pay the price that you are asking. When you can show the public what people are willing to pay on eBay, they will see the value and feel encouraged about and agree to pay the price that you want them to. They will see that it is a *fair* price.

I know of people who make the mistake of allowing themselves to be beaten down on the price, when there are plenty of other buyers who will be happy to pay the price that they are offering. If a buyer really needs what you are offering, or want the product or the service, then as long as you offer them a fair price— even if it is not the cheapest price—and they believe in the quality of what it is that you are offering, they will purchase it. In the end, they will be happy to buy, at that price. You see, you can only go through with this if you are able to show people that you are knowledgeable about the price and not become nervous when people ask for a lower price, and either jump to offer them the lower price, or completely withdraw from the negotiation to offer what it is that you are offering. If you know that it is the right price, the price that you need to insist on in order to make money on eBay then stick with it, as that is one of your goals. You will always want to be able to charge the most that the market will bear for what you are offering.

What also happens many times is that the market price of an item in a certain area is cheaper then it is in other areas. What eBay allows you to do is to focus on selling to those areas where the people will pay the most for your product. What do I mean by that? Say you are set up in the business of selling leather briefcases and you are based in Texas and there is not much of a demand for leather brief-cases, in Texas. You know that people either do not use briefcases or they would rather carry small attachés or small sports bags, but for whatever reason, they do not use briefcases. If you focus on selling to the public in Texas, the people who will buy a leather briefcase from you will know that they have an advantage on their side. They know that since there are very few buyers for that item, they can offer you a very cheap price or you will just have to sell it for a cheap price because nobody really wants your briefcases and the only way they will buy it is if they are getting a great bargain.

Now that same leather briefcase might sell extremely well in Colorado and unless you offer a leather briefcase in Colorado, you will never know that they are willing to buy them, and are willing pay a decent amount of money for one. If you put up an auction on eBay for a leather briefcase, the way that you will know that buyers in Colorado are interested in the product is because you will see where most of your bidders including your highest bidder, come from. Now, if you see the high-est bidder is based in New Mexico and you notice after a few auctions that most of those bidders in your auctions for those leather briefcases are located in New Mexico or Arizona, then you know that the market for that particular merchandise is in those two states or that area of the country. Then you could refocus your business and your whole strategy in selling to consumers in those states. You could begin contacting stores in those states, you could advertise through the mail, and you could put advertisements in magazines or local newspapers in those states. You will save yourself a lot of time and aggravation by being able to focus your product to places where there are actually buyers for your item and where people will be willing to pay the most. Choose those areas where consumers will be willing to pay more then other consumers.

As part of my business, I wholesale adult's and children's socks. I discovered that while in New York the stores did want children's socks, they were happy to buy them in order to resell them, because of course then they had another opportunity to make money in their stores and they would end up paying a lot less then similar stores located right across the border, in New Jersey. When I realized that, I decided to refocus my sales efforts to selling to stores in New Jersey and in other areas of the country because while every store wants to have children's socks to sell to parents who need socks for their children, not every store is willing to pay the same price. You see, in New York, there is an intense amount of competition from wholesalers who are always calling on ninety-nine cent stores, discount stores, and clothing stores to sell them their products, but as you get farther away from New York and farther away from large metropolitan areas, there is less competition on every level. There are less retail stores and fewer wholesalers.

Now the reason there are less wholesalers in rural areas is that there are not enough stores to support more then one or two wholesalers. If you are solely based in your area and have access to the internet, you could use UPS or the U.S. Postal Service to ship boxes to rural areas, then you do not have to rely on the exclusive business from those few small stores in that exclusive area. Even though a wholesaler in Oklahoma might only have fifty or sixty 99 cent stores to sell to, and you are located in another small town, say California, you can use eBay to develop sales and sales leads both in that small town and also in your home town, in California. Using the internet, you have an advantage over the local wholesalers because you will be able to offer a decent price, good merchandise, and you will not have to rely on those few stores in the local area. Once you discover how much easier it is to sell to places outside of large metropolitan areas, you will also become very enthused and want to develop other business lines that will supplement what you are currently selling. You will be able to focus on those stores in the rural areas and make a decent living.

You see, if you live in a metropolitan area, even though you will be facing an intense amount of competition, you will still have a large market to sell to. Say, for example, you have a hundred different wholesalers and a thousand different stores—while even though it will not be split up evenly, the number of stores outnumbers the number of wholesalers—and every wholesaler has the potential to have a decent amount of customers before he loses customers to the next wholesaler. While in reality, the few large wholesalers will have 80% of the marketplace themselves and the smaller wholesalers will have to grasp for the small stores, at which, for whatever reason, they do not buy from the large wholesalers, while there is still enough business for everyone. If you are located in a small area, and are a small wholesaler located in a rural area where there are not many stores, you have a decent challenge. Your challenge is that even though you might be the only one supplying merchandise to this area, there just are not enough stores for your business to grow, let alone creating a successful business that will allow you to retire.

What eBay does, is, it allows you to reach out to the national marketplace, regardless of where you are; whether you are out in a small town in Nebraska or selling an item in an area that no longer desires it. Say you are located in a state with a warm climate, say, in Georgia and you are carrying a winter product. Why do you have that winter product? You got a good deal at an auction, you bought an overstock, because there was a business in another area that went out of business and you bought their remaining inventory. Now you have that merchandise that does not sell well in Georgia. So what do you do? You go ahead and use eBay to start selling that item to stores in other areas where consumers in those areas *need* that merchandise. Say you have a store that carries both summer and winter items and now it is your summer season. So, what do you do with your winter merchandise? You would probably just set it aside in your basement or store it in a storage facility and wait until the next season when you can start selling it. If you use eBay, then you could sell winter merchandise throughout the year and also summer merchandise throughout the year because there will always be areas of the world and country that will be cold and hot.

You could decide to sell overseas, since there are many lucrative opportunities by using eBay to sell overseas. You could take the winter merchandise and sell it to areas in Alaska where it is mostly cold, or sell it to Russia or European countries, during their extended winter season. If you have summer merchandise, you can take that merchandise and sell it to countries in the Middle East, or Southern states, or Latin America. As you can see, there are always opportunities out there for the merchandise that you want to sell or services that you want to offer. The challenge is to find those opportunities and to be able to match yourself with what you have to offer and what people need. When you fulfill those needs, that is when you will start making money with your eBay business.

Chapter 9

Writing a winning auction description is extremely important for your auctions. You see, while many people can put up items on eBay for sale and can write a basic auction description, most people forget about the true value of the written word. The written word entices people's imaginations and excites—it lights the fire that will drive a person to make decisions. The written word can often be more important then the actual visual images. When you write words, you appeal not just to people's desire for the facts and information, you appeal to their emotions and you can guide and show them how this product will fulfill their needs.

You see, people do not buy exercise equipment to get in shape. They buy the exercise equipment to enjoy the benefits of being in better shape—to become healthier, look younger, and to have more energy. So when you write your auction description, say, for exercise equipment, you will want to stress the benefits of getting in shape as opposed to only relying on listing the actual details of the machinery. You want to be able to list both factual information and also to be able to have what people call a sales pitch, where you are selling the item on the benefits it provides on an emotional or physical basis. That is because people do not buy items; they buy solutions to their problems. They look for benefits and fulfillment, and you need to make it very clear through your auction description what it is what you are offering, and how what you are offering will help them.

When you write your auction description, make sure that you use words that are not hard to understand. Many customers do not have a high degree of education and you do not want to turn them away by using words in the description or by writing in a way that they will not understand or that will make them confused. Now, I am not putting anyone down. You do not have be highly educated or have a perfect-sounding vocabulary in order to succeed in business or life, in general. However, since there are people out there who do *not* have a prolific vocabulary; make sure that when you write your auction description that you appeal to them, as well. You want to make sure that they can understand what it is that you are selling and the benefits of what you are offering. When you write your auction description, always make it clear who you are, why people should buy from you, why people should specifically buy the product you are offering, why you are the best source for that product, what the features are for the product or service that you are offering, and the benefits that they will receive.

You should also state some of the benefits other people have received and more importantly, use testimonials provided either by the manufacturer or by the users of the product that receive the product directly from you. Then you will do a good job of convincing people to buy the product or service from you. See, the public wants to know what other peoples' experiences were with what you are offering. This way, they can also feel comfortable in knowing that if they purchase this product or service they will also be able to benefit. People always like to know that there is a third party verifying what you are saying. By third party, they want to know that someone besides yourself, the seller of the product or service, has benefited from the use of it or can verify that the product is of high quality and does offer the benefits that are being stated in the description.

Consumer Reports developed a multimillion-dollar business by becoming a third party verifier for many consumer items, ranging from televisions to appliances to automobiles. Whenever you can use a third party to verify what it is that you are stating or to verify the value and the benefits that you are offering, you will be way ahead of your competition and you will be turning many potential bidders into actual bidders. How can you obtain third party verification? One way to do it is by asking for testimonials from your present and past customers. You could even go to friends or relatives and ask them to try the product in exchange for either giving them a free sample or as a favor if they are happy with what you have given or shown them. Ask them for permission to write down their comments and post their comments on eBay. Now if those testimonials are not legitimate you could get into trouble! If those testimonials are legitimate, even if they are not *serious* testimonials, people will be able to read the comments that people have given.

If you have given someone, for instance, a book to read and the person cannot stop raving about the book as if it is the greatest thing that happened since sliced bread, people will see through that testimonial. On the other hand, if you gave the book to the same friend or relative who wrote a testimonial after they take an honest look at the book and write the reasons why they liked the book and what they felt about the book, then people will say that even though this person might be a relative or friend of the author or seller of the book, from the testimonial they can see that the person's true opinion has probably been stated. It would be even better if you could get testimonials from businesses or organizations that have benefited from the use of the product or service. People like to see that well-known businesses, or organizations have also used what it is that you are offering, and that they are putting their reputation, so to speak, on the line, endorsing what it is that you are offering. If you could have a true endorsement from a company or well-known spokesperson such as a politician, a movie star or a musician, then you will attract many more bidders who will be interested in using your item for two reasons: One reason is because they will know that someone they respect, look up to, or be familiar with, has used and benefited from the product and secondly, they will want to use a product that is associated with that famous person or entity.

Imagine how many people would love to wear the same clothes that a famous movie star wears! Think about how many sneakers Nike is able to sell every year because those sneakers are worn by famous basketball players. If you would like to piggyback on Nike's success, you could offer the same sneakers that Nike sells at retail stores by selling them on eBay. If you could offer these sneakers at a discount compared to what the retail stores charge, you can let people know in your auction description that these sneakers are worn by a certain famous basketball player and you will have people interested in buying the sneakers from you.

If you are selling artwork and you let people know who some of the other buyers of this artwork are, they will also want to buy the artwork if one of the buyers mentioned is a well-known collector, if she is a very famous business woman, if he is a famous politician. Another great endorsement to have could be written by a fellow artist in the field who approves of the art done by this artist or a famous writer who compares another novelist's writings to their own. I am sure you have seen a listing on the back of every paperback book, touting the book by other writers who have enjoyed the book. You will usually find two or three testimonials of other well-known writers who also enjoyed this writer's book. Even if you might not be familiar with the writer of the book, since the book has been endorsed by other well-known writers, you will take the chance. You will say to yourself, "Since I do enjoy this other person's writing style and they are comparing themselves or approves of this person's writing style, chances are I will enjoy the book." You always want to use endorsements when possible.

A good way to get, I would not call it a testimonial, but if you had some extra comments that could help sell the product or service, by contacting the manufacturer and having them write up a special paragraph giving people information on why they would benefit from using this product, that would be helpful. You see, even though the information is coming from the same source, when they see something that is written in a fresh style, which seems to be tailor-made for them, then people will respond differently. You are not asking for a sales pitch from the manufacturer, wholesaler or distributor, you are asking for extra input on the benefits that people can obtain by using this product or service. So while there are many ways to write an auction description, always make sure that you have endorsements, testimonials, and a very effective auction description with a detailed, step-by-step guideline of why this product is a quality product and offers benefits. Make sure to list all of the benefits and go into descriptive detail about the benefits offered and how these benefits fulfill the needs of buyers. Make sure to write from an emotional point of view when you are appealing to the public's emotions and genuine reasons for purchasing the product. If you can do all of this, you should have a very effective auction description that will sell your products at the price you are looking for.

Chapter 10

Have you ever been in a situation where you have bought merchandise, which you just cannot sell? Have you ever made a mistake to purchase a product that would sell for a much higher price then it is actually selling? You are facing the same dilemma that 90% of retailers face at some point in their business. There *are* ways to sell your merchandise. While it will require imagination on your part, it can be done and when done properly, you can actually make more money then if you had sold your merchandise through your originally planned method. The basic premise to sell slow moving merchandise is to take the merchandise and make a list of all the true benefits that merchandise or service can provide for the end user.

If you have fitness equipment, think of every benefit that the equipment can provide for the end user. It can make them feel good about exercise, it can give them something they can do in their own time, it can help them to get in shape, lose weight, become fit, and develop better stamina. What else can exercise equipment do for an end user? It can help them to open up a gym; set up physical rehabilitation or slowly get back into shape. Summer camps can use exercise equipment to provide the staff or campers with another activity. Companies could use the fitness equipment to keep their employees in shape, providing an employee benefit. A nonprofit organization could use the fitness equipment to conduct a raffle for the equipment and use the proceeds of the raffle to raise funds. As you can see, there are many uses for items besides the original intended use for that item.

When you have slow moving merchandise, ask yourself who else can benefit from using this merchandise, this item, or from using your service. If you are selling a service on behalf of someone else, think about the many uses of that service. This process will allow you to open up new channels for the merchandise that you are offering. In the past, you might have only focused on one, two or three types of customers to sell your merchandise to, including specialized merchandise. After you go through this open-minded thought process, you will have a lot more customers and outlets who you can sell your merchandise to. When you look at the example of the fitness equipment, you can see that there are actually many more types of customers that could be interested in your merchandise. You will be able to write auction descriptions matching those customers and their needs and you will be able to sell the merchandise even though it was slow moving, in the first place. If you have some toys, which are now out of style in your area, you could sell those toys to daycare centers that are always looking for a cheap source of toys, which they put out for the children to use. As another example, if you have blank tapes, you could sell them to the student market to students who might want to record lectures given by their professors. You could take the same blank tapes and provide them to people who are in the business of public speaking who want to record themselves to analyze what their speeches sound like to the public, this way they can practice and perfect their abilities in public speaking.

When you go through this entire process and you are able to develop new outlets to sell your merchandise, it allows you to continually be able to sell to these new outlets. As this merchandise starts moving when you sell, you will be able to replenish that same type of merchandise and continue to sell it, now that you have developed new outlets for it—even though originally you might not have wanted to reorder that merchandise because you could not wait to get rid of it and you would be happy to cover your original cost.

Now that you have discovered an effective way to sell that slow moving merchandise at a profit, you could turn around and buy more of it. In many instances, the reason why people have slow moving merchandise is that they got a very good deal on it; the reason they got a good deal is that the person selling the merchandise knew that there really not as many customers for that merchandise as there are for *other* types of merchandise. Say you bought a large amount of pink shoe polish. There are not too many people who need pink shoe polish, but you know who might need it? Professional ballet dancers who wear pink shoes, maybe members of a circus troop. There are people out there who *do* need shoe polish and they might even need other colors. Once you develop a market, and find customers who need pink shoe polish, you could turn around and buy more of it at that same discounted price because you could remind the person selling the shoe polish that there are not very many customers for it.

One of the big secrets to business success is to find merchandise at a price that is very low because of lack of customers for it, and taking that merchandise and rethinking the process of selling it, reevaluating who else can benefit from the merchandise and then gearing your marketing strategy to the public. How do you use eBay to do this? When you write the title, the auction description, and select a category to include the merchandise, you will be reaching out to other types of customers who might use that merchandise. It is not enough just to list that merchandise in a different category, you also have to show the public who are looking in that category, why your merchandise is appropriate for *them*.

Say you have a box of old advertisements from the 1920s. At first glance, you might think there is not much use for a box of old advertisements from the 1920s. How about going to the antique section on eBay and looking under advertising in an attempt to sell those advertisements. Let me say that even though people buy old advertisements for their antique appeal or collectible appeal, for the sake of argument, no one wants to buy these specific advertisements. So what can you do now? Think of who else might benefit from using those advertisements. How about an advertising agency that is always looking for new ideas? While an advertisement from the 1920s is not new, it can be new to someone who has not seen that add and can either copy that add or obtain ideas from that add, then go ahead and use them for his new advertising strategy. Who else can use those advertisements from the 1920s? How about an antique store? They could put up the ads on the wall and give the store more of an antique look. What about a restaurant? The restaurant could add some "flavor" to the interior design by placing the 1920s advertisements on the walls. How would you reach a restaurant owner through eBay? Go to the restaurant section and list your item under supplies. Explain in your auction description how great it would be for a restaurant owner to be able to put up these 1920s ads on his walls and explain how much the customers might enjoy eating in a restaurant while they are checking out these interesting, original ads that have not been repeated since the 1920s. Every restaurant owner knows that the longer they can keep their customers sitting at the table, the more food and drinks they will order and the more business they will have. Therefore, the key is to look at the product from a different angle and to squeeze out as many possibilities for selling that item. How about an extremely hard product to sell?

What about the product, clown shoes? There are many clowns are out there, maybe a thousand, maybe two thousand? It would be safe to say that those clowns are already buying their shoes from certain sources or maybe the circuses themselves are purchasing the shoes for the clowns. You could try to sell your clown shoes to the circuses, maybe to the suppliers of the circuses, or you could sell shoes to the clowns directly, however maybe that market is already saturated or the clowns do not specifically need those types of circus shoes you are offering. Who could you offer the circus shoes to? How about actors in plays? If an actor is going to have a role as a clown and they need clown shoes, they might not know where to find them. How about schools that put on productions? What about a nonprofit organization that is going to be putting on a party and plans to have one of their members dress up as a clown? What about a festival? How about a flea market that wants to have a clown to entertain customers? How about a retail store that wants to have an in-store promotion for children to give out balloons or entertain the kids? As you can see, there are many uses for those clown shoes, it is just a matter of thinking how to properly market your product.

There is always a way to market slow moving merchandise. Practicing this philosophy, there is no such thing as slow moving merchandise; instead, there is the ability to discover who needs the product and to market to those customers. Sometimes, even if you know who might best benefit from your product, you might not know how to reach those people. They will not know you have the product in the first place and if you do not know how to explain to those people how they can benefit from the products that you are offering, and they will not see the value, they will not use your product. If you can reach the public, and eBay allows you to reach millions and millions of people, especially when you allow international bidders to purchase your items, you are in-like-flint. When you develop the skills to write an ad based on an emotional basis, and show what emotions and needs can be fulfilled through the acquisition of what you are offering, then you will have a very good chance of selling the merchandise and the services to the marketplace.

Chapter 11

An eBay auction has a lot of potential and unless you know how to release the full potential of your eBay auction, you will be missing out on a lot of business that could be yours. You see, there are many benefits besides the obvious benefit of selling the item or service that you are advertising. There are many more ways to make money that are not apparent, and once you examine what an auction can do for you and if you look beneath the surface, you will discover many more opportunities. One opportunity that I like to refer to as a back-end sale, is when someone wins your auction, give him or her the opportunity to purchase more merchandise from you. Let them know that you have more of the same merchandise available and if they would like more units then they have already purchased, by being the top bidder at the auction, let them know that you have that merchandise available for them.

For instance, if somebody bought a pair of shoes through your auction, when the auction is over, let them know that besides that pair of shoes that they purchased from you, you can sell them more shoes. Now if you are auctioning off a collectable or a very hard-to-find item, you do not want to tell that person that you have a good deal more copies of the same thing because then they will regret that they paid so much, if the item is really not rare. So if you are auctioning off a comic book from 1965, say it is an original Spider Man, and the first issue that Spider Man ever appeared in. You do not want to let the top bidder know that you have another five of the same comic books because they will not see the value in what they just purchased. Even though in actuality it is a very valuable item, when you are auctioning off an item that is mass-produced and more widely available, you can let the winning bidder know that you have more of the same item(s) and that you could offer them additional items at a discounted price. For instance, if somebody wins a pack of 100 batteries through an auction with you, you could offer that winner an additional twenty batteries at a discounted price. This way, aside from the original sale that is done through the auction, you can also make more money by selling them more batteries—and this can be done with any product or service. If, for instance, you auctioned off the preparation of a tax return, you can offer that person an additional year of tax preparation at a discounted price if they prepay now. This way you have made more money through the same auction.

Another way to do a back-end sale and to make money, is to offer someone a similar product. For instance, someone bids on a subscription to a one-year magazine to *Forbes*. Once they win that auction and pay for their one-year subscription to *Forbes*, you could also offer them a one-year subscription to *Business Week*, *Entrepreneur*, *Inc.*, or any other business magazine that you have access to. This way, you are making more money from the same sale. Studies have shown people who make purchases, after they have paid for their purchase, they are 50% more likely to make another purchase from the same seller, as long as the merchandise is offered to them within a very short period of time of their original purchase. So if you can, show them another item for sale immediately after the auction is completed. After they have paid for the item, you have a very good chance to turn them into a buyer who will purchase more items from you. Again, there are many ways to obtain additional revenue.

Now I am going to show you another way. Look through the list of all the high bidders for your auction. High bidders are the top two-or-three bidders for the item that you auctioned off. Contact the non-wining top bidders. Look at the top three-or-four bidders and contact all the bidders who have not won the item from you and offer them the same or similar product at the price that the top bidder won the item for. Many times even though they were not willing to bid that much for the item, maybe the top bid for the item was $100. Even if the second-highest bidder did not bid $100. for the item, when they are approached with a second chance to purchase the item, they might be interested in purchasing that item. The eBay site allows you to send a second chance offer to that bidder or any bidder that the seller desires. When you send a second chance offer, what happens is the bidder can purchase the item for the top bid. But if you want them to spend more money, then contact them directly, send them an e-mail, and then you could either sell them the item for the price that you want or compromise and sell them the item for more then they actually bid, but less then what the actual top bidder bid on the item. Now you would do this when you have more then the same item and you could also do this in any situation where you want to move volume. This way, you are opening up more opportunities to sell merchandise. Now, if you are having a very easy time selling your merchandise, you might not want to contact any of the other bidders because they might end up paying less, because they know they can just wait for the next auction. The flip-side of that, is, if you can sell the item very easily through the auction process, then do not contact any of the bidders and just wait for the next auction, create another auction, write a good item description, and just wait for another top bidder to buy the item from you. If you have a very large quantity of items of the same thing, then I would recommend contacting the bidders.

Another way to make money from your auctions is to keep a list of every inquiry of each person who called or e-mailed regarding the auction and contact them after the sale is completed. Offer to sell them the same or similar items in your possession. Even though they might pay less than what the top bidder paid, remember that eBay takes a small percentage of the sale, as a fee. So if you sold the bidder an item for $100., say you sold them a rare record player, eBay will take approximately 3% of the final price. They will take that amount and charge it to your fee. You are actually, in effect, making only $97 instead of $100. If you sell a similar record player to a person who sent you an inquiry for $97 or $95, you do not have to give eBay 3% of the sale, because you are conducting business on your own terms, at that point, by responding to calls and e-mails outside of eBay. You do not have to pay a listing fee and you will not do not have to wait the time that it takes to go through the auction process, to receive payment, or to wait to mail out the product. Again, there are many ways to make money through your eBay auction.

Another way is to offer additional products or services within the same auction. You could list in your auction that you have large quantities available at discounted prices. Therefore, when a person looks at your auctions, and they are looking at an auction for books, and they are considering a collection or small group of a hundred books, let them know that you have larger quantities available. Then if there is an interested book buyer, perhaps they have a large store or they are a wholesaler and interested in buying in quantities of a thousand or more. You could let them know that you have larger quantities, they can contact you, and you can make a deal with them directly, allowing them to purchase books straight from you.

You can also offer consulting services in your auction. You could let the public know that you are available to consult on a personal one-on-one basis for whatever it is that you are involved in, whether it is the book business, art business, clothing business, or the antique business. You could also offer them consulting on selling on eBay regardless what product it is that they are selling, and by selling on eBay and demonstrating that you are a successful eBay seller, the public will want your advice, and people will want to gain from your experience on eBay and be happy to pay you to learn from you. You should always list in all of your auctions your availability for consulting and teaching people how to set up their own eBay businesses.

Chapter 12

If you are familiar with eBay, and have spent time looking through eBay, you will notice a new feature that eBay has added this past year. That feature is the *buy-it-now* option. The *buy-it-now* option allows you to set up an option on your auction that will allow people viewing the auction to instantly purchase the item you have for auction instead of waiting for the entire auction process and other bidders to come on board or waiting three or four days for the auction to be completed. It allows the buyer or the potential buyer who is looking at your auction to go to the auction, bid on the auction, and actually purchase the item instantly.

For instance, say you have a watch for sale on an auction and you set a seven-day time period on the auction. Now, in those seven days, anyone could come into the auction and bid. If you have a feeling that the auction is going to end up at a certain price, you could use the *buy-it-now* feature for that price. If you believe that the final auction price will be around ten dollars, or say $75. for a more expensive watch, you can set the *buy-it-now* feature for $75. Then if anyone wants that watch and they are willing to pay $75. on the spot before the auction is finalized, you can go ahead and give that option and the bidder can go ahead and pay $75. by keying on the link that says "*buy-it-now.*" Instantly, a PayPal or credit card page will open up and they can enter their information or they can agree to send payment through the methods that you allow, whether it is a money order, a check, a cashier's check, a U.S. Postal money order or PayPal; you decide. Now, a *buy-it-now* feature has many options and benefits.

One major benefit is that it allows a bidder that is interested in the item to purchase the item right then and there. Why is it a good feature to use for the seller? You have an interested bidder and that bidder definitely wants that watch, and you know what? Over the course of the next five or six days, until the auction is over, that bidder might lose interest or might not just lose interest, the bidder might have other things going on in their life and they could forget about the auction. So, while they are definitely interested in winning that auction and put

68

in a bid at the time, they might forget about the auction when it actually comes near to completion. So say that bidder is willing to bid as high as $75. and currently the price of that auction is $15. He might put in a bid for $20., even though he might be willing to go as high as $75. However, four days later, when the auction is completed, he or she might not be near their computer. What will happen is, even though they are willing to purchase that item, they were not by their computer for whatever reason, and they will not be able to place a bid on your auction. Maybe they have an errand to do, or perhaps the auction ends late at night or early in the morning, or for some reason they cannot pull themselves away from their work, or from the task that they are currently doing. You might wonder why that person did not place a bid for $75. You see, the reason could be that the person might not *want* to buy it for $75., if they feel they have a chance to buy it for the $20. bid or they might be interested in following the auction until it closes, or lastly, this particular person might not have thought of that option. They might say to themselves, yes I am willing to pay spend $75. for that watch, but if the auction is simply pricing it at $20. now, why should I spend more? If you present the *buy-it-now* feature for $75., you are telling the bidder you know that chances are, you are going to get $75. for the watch or the watch will go beyond that *buy-it-now* price.

Once a bidder sees that you have a *buy-it-now* feature for $75., their assumption will be—and their assumption should be correct—you are willing to accept less than what you expect it to go for, if someone agrees to buy it immediately. You need to make sure that this assumption will be correct by analyzing what it is that you have for sale, so their assumption will be that the item will go beyond $75. and therefore, why would the bidder expect you to take less than this? The bidder might not want to wait a full seven days for the auction to end and then have to make arrangements for the seller to receive their payment, and the seller is willing to take less then he actually expects the auction to end at, as long as he receives payment now. Therefore, the *buy-it-now* feature, the *buy-it-now* option, makes sense to the bidder because they might say to themselves, Look, this makes sense! The seller is willing to accept less, but they are getting their money now. And the flip-side to that, is, a bidder is looking at your auction—that is, if there is a *buy-it-now* feature for $75.—and that means when the auction is completed after seven days, the actual final auction bidding price and winning bid will be higher then $75.

You see, a *buy-it-now* feature is a good solution to the problem of an interested bidder simply being away from the computer when the auction is done. If that interested bidder will be leaving and not by the auction at the time when it ends, you are giving them an option to purchase the item immediately at the price that they are willing to spend. Now, the question is, as a winning bidder, if they end up buying it for $75. or more, then why, as a seller, would you be interested in having the item up for sale with a *buy-it-now* option, which might be less then the final winning bid? One reason, as was stated, is if you want to end the sale early and receive your money immediately, instead of waiting seven days, then you would want to use the *buy-it-now* feature, allowing any bidder to bid before the auction is over. The winning bidder would then gain, because they are able to buy the item without having to wait for the sale to end and you, as the seller, would gain, because you also would not have to wait for the entire auction to end before you received your money.

The reason why I would never recommend to have a *buy-it-now* feature on one of your auctions, unless you are dealing with a specific situation, is because you will be eliminating what could be a much more profitable auction. You see, if you let an auction run its natural course, you will have many new bidders coming on board as it nears its completion, including the last day, the last twelve-hour period and the last one-hour period. You would be surprised how many more bidders will come on board and how many *more* bids that it will produce. Think of how competitive the bidding will be for an item that is desirable during the last hour of its completion. Therefore, you want to make sure that you can allow people to come on board during the last twelve hours and the last hour. If you use a *buy-it-now* feature, you will not allow many of those bidders who will wait until the last minute to bid and come on board.

The reason many wait for the last minute is that they want to avoid building up the price. If you bid $10. for an item and I bid $15. on the same item, then the lowest possible bid that someone else can place is $15.50. However, if you and I had waited until the last minute to bid, then the lowest bid would still be $10. because no one was able to bid higher then that as there had not yet been a bid for $10. They can place *their* bid, and as long as you do not place your bid for $10. or $15., you have not increased the base for which the next bidding level would start. Even though there are many people who will wait, everything will continue compounding and building itself up on the next bid, as long as there is plenty of time left through which more bidders can come on board. Now, all the last minute bidders can substantially push up the price of an auction up because it is not just one or two bidders. In many instances, sometimes there can be ten or fifteen bidders waiting with the same strategy to bid at the last minute in hopes of acquiring the item without having to face much of the competition they would face, otherwise.

Sometimes, waiting for the last minute to bid on an item, the bidders are hoping to send a signal to other people that this is not an item worth bidding on and that is why the current price is so low. The highest price that has been bid is so low because no one is interested and then by sending others the signal that this is not an item worth bidding on, hopefully they will discourage people and can come in at the last minute and purchase the item with a low bid. Either way, what you can see, is there are many bidders who wait until the last day, or until the last twelve hours and place their bid within the last hour. A *buy-it-now* feature eliminates this process.

Now there are times when you will want to use the *buy-it-now* feature, when the item is a very commonly available item that you are hoping to sell simply by being able to offer it at a very low price. If the item is being offered for $30. in most retail outlets and most eBay sellers are selling it with a minimum starting bid of $15., then you are looking to sell that item at $10. Suppose at $10. you can still make money out of your purchase cost. Then you would want to use the *buy-it-now* feature and allow the public to purchase the item at $10. This way when all the bidders see that the item is being sold elsewhere for $20. or $30. and they see they can purchase it from you for $10., they would most probably be inclined to use the *buy-it-now* feature, because they will be able to purchase the item quickly, without having to wait.

In that situation you will not mind, because even if the item goes up to $20., you will already be facing competition from all of the other eBay sellers and if you can establish a good profit for yourself, then why not allow someone to buy it instantly? This way you can make yourself a fair profit and if you have a lot of the same item, such as in a situation where you might have a hundred DVD players that originally retailed for $200 and are selling on eBay for $150. If you purchased those DVD players at a cost of $50 a piece, you might be very happy to offer a *buy-it-now* feature for $100. That way, the public will become excited when they see your price and they will decide to buy it right away without waiting for the auction to end because you are already offering your items for such a good price. They might not want to take the chance of losing the opportunity to purchase a DVD player, which normally retails for $200., at $100. You do not mind selling it quickly without having to wait for the auction process to close, even though you might have actually received more then $100. because since you have a hundred pieces, you will be making your money in volume. If you sell a hundred pieces using the *buy-it-now* feature over the course of a month or the course of two months and make $50. profit on each piece, you will be making $5,000. So even though you could have made maybe $6,000. or $7,000. by waiting over a three-or four-month period, you now have $5,000. which you can reinvest in your business, take out and enjoy the profits and/or reinvest the rest of the money back into your business.

So, you always have to make a decision, are you looking for volume or are you looking to make your money per piece? If you are looking to make your money on volume, you will have many of the same items and are willing to sell the items for a very low price. Moreover, that price will still give you a good profit, but if it is much lower than what the other sellers are offering the same item for; then it could be a good situation to use the *buy-it-now* feature.

Chapter 13

Writing an important headline is extremely important for your eBay auction. The first thing that someone sees when he or she looks at your auction description is the headline. They look at that headline even before they have an opportunity to see the description. You see, there is no way for them to skip the headline and look at the description as they are able to do with a newspaper advertisement. Even when someone goes to a web site, he or she could quickly browse through the web site without looking at the headline that comes before the text.

You see, the reason that takes place is when you go to eBay and look at all the listings, you will notice the way the listings are displayed by their headlines. If you go to a certain category and you type in the word "tents," for instance, you will see a listing of all the different auctions that have the word "tent" in them. If you look at a category, even if you look at a category such as old baseball cards, and you look at all the listings, you will see a listing of auctions. How are the auctions listed? They are listed by headlines, and when you scroll down to the end of the page, click on a certain category, and then look at that category, you will see throughout the category the listings are set up according to the names the headlines have been given. So instead of someone actually being able to see a short summary instantly, of what the item is, and then making a decision based on that summery whether they should bid on the item or not, the only thing that you can see when you examine the categories are the headlines.

Now, eBay also allows you to add a gallery picture, where you can see a small picture of the item alongside the headline, and those pictures are usually so small, that what attracts the attention of a bidder to your listing is the headline that you use. The headline will also be the first thing people see once they click on your listing. Therefore, the headline is extremely important, especially when there is a category that has a lot of competition, and pretty much any item now on eBay has a lot of competition. When there is a lot of competition, you need to do whatever you can to make your item stand out. While having a picture, as was stated earlier, next to the headline, is very important and also helps, the biggest selling point to get someone to take the first step and to click on your listing and then to look at your auction, is having a very powerful and attention-grabbing headline.

So what kind of headline will get someone's attention to come to your auction? To begin with, the headline has to be captivating and exciting, to draw someone's attention. The best way to do that is by appealing to the public's curiosity. You want people to be so curious about what you are offering that they will not want to *wait* to look at your listing. Personally, I do not want the public to look at other people's listings and then say, "OK, once I have gone through the other listings, then I will arrive at Donny Lowy's listing, and have a chance to look at his auction." No, what I want is to make my headline so exciting that people will have almost no choice, but to click on my auction first—and examine my listing. Once I have them on my auction, then I have a good chance of having them bid—and not only do I want their bid, I want them to concentrate on my auction because hopefully they will be so excited about my auction, they will ignore other people's auctions.

See, if people look at my auction and they are not so excited, they will leave and go to someone else's auction. And if I have given them a great headline that draws them in, keeps them excited and encourages them to bid on my auction, it reduces the chances of them even wanting to look at someone else's auction and they will hopefully be exclusively devoted toward bidding on my auctions. So how can you make a headline powerful and get people so curious that they are going to want to click on it? You need to use words that elicit the emotions that you want. If you want someone to be curious, you could use the word secret in your headline. When you use the word secret, people will want to know what your secret is.

Another way that you can get people curious and excited at the same time, use the word amazing, or you could use the word new, people are always curious about what is new and if it is new, then it must be something good, it must be something interesting. How about this for a headline, "AMAZING & NEW DISCOVERY WILL HELP YOU LOSE WEIGHT!" It is something "NEW," so people have not tried before, it is "AMAZING," so it must work wonders and you could even use the phrase "AMAZING SECRET DISCOVERY!" or "NEW, AMAZING SECRET DISCOVERY!" Something to get people excited, curious, and something that will show people it will be fulfilling an emotion. Say you are auctioning off a used car, a 1989 Lincoln Cadillac. While it is a used car, I would personally not say it is amazing or exciting and that there is probably not much to be curious about it, yet what if your headline read, "DISCOVER THE SECRET REASON PEOPLE LOVE OLD CADILLACS!" In your auction description, you give reasons why people love Cadillacs; such as why Cadillac enthusiasts are devoted to the brand. What you are doing is giving people a reason to be excited, you are creating curiosity about the car you are offering and hopefully you will draw them in. I once read of a master marketer who wrote a sixteen-page sales letter, did not have any pictures included in the sales letter, did not use any testimonials, yet he used this sales letter to sell his golf clubs for $1,600. If you can sell golf clubs for $1,600., without having to use any pictures or any testimonials, simply using a letter, then you could definitely do the same with eBay.

What is another way to make your headline very eye-grabbing and appealing? Use the word "free" in it. When you use the word "free" (everyone wants something for free), you draw people in. You can try this in your headline, "FREE BONUS INCLUDED IN THIS AUCTION!" or "BETTER THAN FREE!" People will be drawn into the auction because they will want to know what could be better than free. Now remember, you do not want to mislead the public, you always want to make sure that your headline is based on the reality of what you are offering. However, if you can take that reality and make it sound exciting enough for people to want to try it out, then you will be doing a really good job and people will be coming to your auction and looking forward to seeing what other types of auctions you have.

The eBay site also allows you to set your headline in bold. You could have the whole headline in bold and you could highlight, it as well. The eBay site has found that having your auction headline in bold and highlighted can boost the actual number of visitors who come to your auction and they found that the average auction that uses a bold and highlighted headline received higher bids than a similar auction that did not use those two features. For these reasons, I highly recommend that your headline be set in bold and highlighted. Together, it costs about $6. to have those features set up. If you are selling something where your profit will be at a *minimum* over $10., then I would suggest that you spend the $6. extra. That way, if you know you are going to be making $10., you have $6. to cover your cost out of the $10. profit and at the same time, you can increase that $10. profit to at least $15. or $20. by attracting more bidders to your auction. Again, the more bidders you have at your auction, the higher your price can go. Anything you can do, including the headline, to make your auction that much more interesting, will draw bidders in and will, hopefully, give you a much higher final winning bid, which results in more money in your pocket.

Chapter 14

When you go through the listing process on eBay, you will notice that one of the options you are allowed to select is how long you want the auction to run. You can select the auction to run for a three-day period, a five-day period, or a seven-day period and for an additional ten cents charge, you could have your auction running for ten days. When you submit all the options for the listings, there are different listing fees and there is an extra ten cents fee if you want your auction to run for ten days. Otherwise, you can select to run the auction for three, five, seven, or ten days. So the question is, how long should you run your auction?

One of the biggest questions when it comes to having an auction on eBay is, by having a shorter auction, do you put more pressure and competition on the bidders and produce a higher bid? On the other hand, in having a longer auction, do you allow more time for new bidders to come in and push up the price, as their bids are added to the bids that are already placed by the people who have been following the auction? The simple way would be to compromise, instead of making it a three-day auction, or a ten-day auction, perhaps one time make it a five-day auction and another time make it a seven-day auction. The reason that solution does not work is because a three-day auction produces very different results for different products than a seven-day auction would, for other products.

See, if you have an auction that is taking place due to an event and you are looking to capitalize on something that is happening in the media or in life, currently, that is what makes your auction *very exciting*. Then you might want to make a very, very short auction, such as a three-day auction and have a *buy-it-now* feature, so that people who are excited about what's going on in the media will most probably want to partake in the fad or craze for a certain collectible and jump on the opportunity to win your auction. If, on the other hand, you have something up for sale that is not directly related to a current event, then you are not as constrained by the time factor.

Say, for instance, they made an Elvis Presley movie and a lot of people who otherwise would not have collected Elvis Presley in the past, are really excited. They are looking to buy up all types of Elvis Presley collectibles in the hope that once the movie comes out, the value of all Elvis Presley collectibles will sky rocket in value. You want to capitalize on the anticipation and the increase in price for collectibles that is already taking place due to the rush of new collectors and new investors looking to make money off those collectibles. So what do you do, in that situation? You would probably want to have an auction for a very, very short period of time; while the craze or fad is taking place and there is a lot of excitement, desire, and interest to purchase Elvis Presley collectibles. While the craze is taking place, the public will come on board, look at your auction, bid it up, and hopefully buy it.

If, on the other hand, you are auctioning off a collectible, which always seems to be in steady demand, and say you find an antique. You have an old chest set from the early 1800s, and that chest set will appeal to two groups. One group will be antique collectors and the other will be people who are chest enthusiasts who would love to have a chest set from the early 1800s. With an item like that, you want to give it as much time as possible to attract attention from different bidders and you also want people who are bidding for the auction to have plenty of time to compete against each other. Therefore, you should make it a ten-day auction. The difference is, with the Elvis Presley collectible, if you make the auction too long, there is a chance that in a few days, the pent-up desire for Elvis Presley collectibles could dissipate and you will be left holding on to that collectible without having been able to sell it for a decent price.

If you have an item where there is a steady amount of interest and it is not dependent on an event that is taking place, then you have more time to auction it off. Another example would be if you are auctioning off a used car and the mileage of the car is not going to be changing anymore because you are not driving it. Then you want to give that auction as much time to run so that the public can find the auction, bid on it, and the competition for that item will build. On the other hand, say you have a bottle of wine that is champagne and the champagne, as I have been told, is best served when it is eighteen years old and if it is getting close to its nineteenth birthday, then you want to make the auction is as short as possible. This way you do not take any chance of getting close to that nineteenth birthday. Especially, and this does happen sometimes, the highest bidder drops out and does not pay for the auction and you are forced to re-list the item. If that happens you are going to be under a lot of pressure due to the time that is running out.

Another example is if you are auctioning off vitamins and the vitamins have an expiration date coming up in another ten weeks; so the vitamins are still good for the next ten weeks and someone who uses them can enjoy them until their freshness date expires. Now, since you have a very limited amount of time, you want to make it a very short auction. You want people to say to themselves, "It is a three-day auction and even after waiting two or three days to have it delivered, I can still use these vitamins for the next few weeks. It is worthwhile for me to purchase these vitamins at a highly discounted price even though the expiration date is coming soon."

Another item where you would want to have a ten-day auction or if eBay allows you to have an even longer auction period, would be if you were auctioning off a business. If you are auctioning off a business, the business will be there; it is not disappearing. The interest for a business is not based on a fad, it is based on the public's interest to be in business and to make more money then they are currently making. Therefore, with a business, you will want to give it time to attract as many bidders as possible and you will want to give the public time while the auction is taking place. You do not want them to feel pressured; they should feel that they have the opportunity to call you up to discuss the business with you, to research the business and then place their bid. If it is a three-day auction there is no way that people will be able to feel that they have done all the research that they need before the auction is finalized. Many people will become, I would not say discouraged, but they might be turned-off at being forced to make a decision in such a short period of time over what could be an expense of thousands and thousands of dollars. So they would hesitate to even bid on that auction, and they might just ignore it, instead.

Although, if you give people a ten-day auction, then during that ten-day window of opportunity they can call you up, call the references that you have given, and then they can decide if your business is really for them. Now, according to that logic, you might say that it really does not pay to auction off a business at all, on eBay. Why put something up for auction where people might become unmotivated to want to bid in the auction due to the time constraints that they have? The reason I think that eBay is a perfect place to auction a business is because when you sell something at an auction, people know that at some point time will run out and they will not be able to purchase the business, in this case, again. They know that they have to make a decision and they have to make it *now*. If it is for them, they know that if they do not act on the opportunity and bid and try to win this business, they will have missed out on a great opportunity. Ten days is a good amount of time to investigate it.

See, when a business is sold through a business broker or through more commonly accepted methods, what happens is that the public has months and months to negotiate, to research a business and if a better deal comes up, they will switch to the next deal. They will investigate that deal, and if that deal does not pan out, then they will return to your business, which is for sale, and they will spend a lot of time negotiating and looking around. They can actually even use the fact that there might not be other people interested in your business as a negotiating tactic, but if you go ahead and set a ten-day auction and the public knows that if they do not make their decision in ten days, they will have missed out on the opportunity to have this business. This will also force them to make a decision and will put more leverage on your side. Because even if people call you up and try to negotiate with you, you could tell them that there are other bidders who are interested and if in ten days they do not put in a bid, they are out of luck! You will simply have to sell the business to someone else. Therefore, in an item such as a business, I would recommend that you go ahead and select a ten-day auction period so you allow people to investigate the auction and at the same time, it forces people to act on it and make their decision earlier. Especially if you are going to go ahead and auction off a large ticket item, such as a business or a car, then you can definitely afford to spend an extra ten cents to extend the duration of the auction.

Chapter 15

Learning how to run an auction on eBay and learning what you can do to make your auction appealing and successful, is half of the battle. Like the old cartoon says, "There is another half to the battle and that half to the battle is knowing what mistakes to avoid." You need to know, especially when you run a business, the biggest mistakes that sellers do, to turn off bidders. These are: high handling fees, high shipping costs, high opening bids, low feedback or negative feedback, poor quality pictures, bad grammar, and vague auction descriptions. I will talk about each one.

First, I am sure that you realize that the public, in looking at an auction, are looking at the auction similar to an advertisement they would see in a newspaper, magazine, on TV, or the radio. They realize that the seller is most probably engaged in a business and because of that fact, on one hand, the buyer thinks they need to be more careful, and might worry over what it is that they are purchasing from you and the transaction they are entering with you. On the other hand, since they know you are in business, they expect certain standards from you. If you do not meet those standards, they will not see you as a legitimate businessperson and they might not want to conduct business with you. If you want to make sure to have customers and a long-term relationship with those customers as repeat buyers, which are the lifeblood of any business, then you need to make sure to avoid the worst mistakes eBay sellers make.

Let me explain the first mistake; high handling fees. A handling fee is a fee that sellers charge people for putting together their auction and sending it out. You see, buyers do not like to see that handling fee, even though they realize that it is going to take some effort on your part to pack your belongings and mail them out or to pack your merchandise and ship it out to them and that is part of doing business. When they work on their jobs or when they run their own businesses, they do not charge for many services. For example, if they are a wholesaler and they are delivering socks to a store, they do not charge the store a delivery charge, they simply pack up the socks into a van, deliver the socks to the vendor, and then charge the storeowner for the socks. Their money is made from the profit of the socks. Bidders or buyers on eBay, have also seemed to have come to the conclusion that they do not mind a seller making money off of the items that they are selling, but their profit should be restricted to the actual cost of the item minus or plus what is paid for. Therefore, if an item costs the seller $10. and the bidding goes up to $25., and the buyer realizes that they will have to pay for shipping and handling, they might find it insulting that on top of profit that you made, they have to pay an additional handling charge. While it might look fair on your part, the customer is king (or queen), especially on an eBay business; you will want to make sure to keep your customer happy, especially if you want the customer to come back and make a second or third purchase from you. So avoid handling fees at all costs. If you find that it is just not worthwhile to sell merchandise without charging a handling fee, then you should look at selling a different type of product that gives you a higher profit margin.

The next big mistake is high shipping costs, and the shipping cost can be avoided. Shipping costs is just part of doing business and buyers realize that; however buyers can become extremely suspicious if they see a very high shipping cost that does not reflect the reality based on what they have paid in similar situations. Remember, chances are that the buyer has already bought similar items from other sellers and if those other sellers charge for $25. shipping and you are looking to charge $50., that buyer will become very suspicious and might not even complete the transaction with you, even if later on you offer to lower the shipping fee. I will suggest from the beginning to find out the cheapest way to ship the merchandise, and if the buyer balks at such a high shipping cost, if your profit allows it, subsidize the shipping. Offer to pay some money toward the shipping. This way the person who has bought the merchandise from you will feel that you have actually gone a step further, in subsidizing the shipping, and to make it cheaper for him. Plus, you can look at the amount of shipping out of your own pocket as a business expense. You could say to yourself, "OK, the cost for the item I sold for $50. is no longer $10.; it is now $15. because I had to put $5. toward the shipping." I think it is worth it, because you have secured yourself a good, loyal customer who is always going to remember how you took care of them by paying for some of the shipping. At the same time, the sale went through successfully; and you have pocketed the profit that you made, minus the additional cost of the shipping that you paid for.

Another mistake that sellers make that must be avoided is allowing themselves to receive negative feedback. The feedback system allows sellers and buyers to look at each other's feedback and to see how other members of eBay have rated this person when they have conducted transactions with this individual. They can see if the seller or buyer has received negative feedback, reporting why the other person was unsatisfied with the transaction. A neutral report is one where the person was not thrilled with the transaction, yet they are still not satisfied enough to give the person positive feedback. Positive feedback is where the person is actually happy that they conducted the transaction with the other eBay member. The way to avoid having negative feedback is by making sure to always engage in a legitimate and honest transaction and to go ahead and do your best to resolve any situations before the buyer or seller gives you negative feedback. If one of the parties you are dealing with is not happy, ask what it is that you can do to make it up to him or her and see what it is you can do to make them a satisfied customer. Many times, all it takes to make the other party comfortable is just expressing yourself with sincerity, communicate properly and to let the person know that you are willing to work with him or her, and that you are willing to do whatever it takes to make them a satisfied customer. Communication by itself can help you receive positive feedback in a situation where instead, you might have received negative feedback and, of course, your communications and your sentiments have to be backed by action. You have to make sure that you will be delivering something positive for the seller or buyer as the situation calls for.

Low feedback could also be a problem. Low feedback arises even when you have received only positive feedback, and yet there are too few instances of feedback. If you only have two or three kinds of feedback in your profile history, people might be weary to do business with you, whether you are looking to buy or sell because they just simply do not know enough about you, to trust you. The way to handle this situation where you have low feedback, is to engage in as many transactions as a buyer, complete the transactions, pay for the transactions and then ask the seller to leave you positive feedback. You can buy a lot faster then you can sell. If you buy five items and complete the transactions, and you are satisfied with what you have done and the seller feels good about doing business with you, then you can receive five positive feedback. In the past, you would have had to wait a long time before you sold five different items and received positive feedback from each of those buyers. Another thing you can do while you have low feedback, if you do not want to buy anything or if you have already bought merchandise and still want to increase your appearance, is to write a lot of information about yourself in your auction description. Talk about what it is that you do—you could put testimonials in the description and you can also let people know that you have references available upon request. This way, people will feel comfortable knowing that there are people who you did business with, who are satisfied, and if they need to contact them, they will have that option.

Using poor quality pictures can be a discouragement to bidders. Using a poor quality picture can sometimes be worse then not having any picture at all. If you do not have a picture in your auction description, they still might bid on the item and you might receive a decent bid. It would not be that bad, because people can use their imagination and if it is a product that they are familiar with or a product that they do not need to see a picture for, it still could sell. Of course having a good quality picture works the best and will most likely work in your favor, but if you only have access to a lesser quality digital camera or a poor quality picture, avoid the situation by using the picture and taking the chance of turning off bidders. Instead, do not have a picture at all. Now, not having a picture is not always the best substitute for having a poor quality picture. Your goal should be to have a good quality picture. How do you do that? You go ahead and purchase yourself a good digital camera or at the beginning ask a friend or a professional photographer take pictures for you.

Now one thing I mentioned that turns bidders away on eBay, is having a poorly written auction description. By poorly written, I am talking about vague, so the public does not know what it is that you are selling, or do not clearly understand why they should purchase it from you. If it is vague enough, people will even become suspicious that you are trying to hide information or, God forbid, you are trying to mislead them. Another mistake that people make, which does happen very often and is really no fault of the seller, is using bad grammar in describing your auction. The public will simply say that it is not professional, this seller does not seem educated, and they will not bid on your auction. Even if it is something they really want, if they see bad grammar in the auction description or they do not see an auction description that has not been written so that they understand it, they will say to themselves that probably the merchandise is just at the same quality as the auction description, right? They will connect both of them because they are both being produced by the same person. The person writing the auction description is the same person who will be selling them the merchandise. You do not want to turn them off by having bad grammar and leaving them to believe that the quality of your business is as poor as the grammar or style of your auction description.

That matter can be resolved easily by having a friend, a relative, a teacher, a college student, or an editor proofread your auction before you put it up on eBay—and getting a second opinion never hurts! Having a second opinion allows you to have the clarity of mind and to know beyond a reasonable doubt whether you have done a good job on writing a good, solid auction description or not. In addition, when you show your auction description to someone else, you will know besides the question of whether the grammar is good or not, you will also know if you have written the auction in a way that appeals to people. If you show the auction description to a friend of yours who loves fishing and they read the auction description and suggests to you, "Well, your grammar is great, but I just really would not want to buy what's being offered in this auction." Then, you realize that either the merchandise is either of poor quality, which is good to know because the next time you could sell something else—or you know the merchandise is good and offered at a very cheap price—that the auction description, although the grammar may be correct, does not live up to the product that you are trying to sell. It always helps to have a second opinion and hopefully done by someone who has a very good grasp on the English language. If you can avoid these mistakes, you will be on your way to setting up a successful eBay business that can produce good revenues for you and your family. Remember, it is not always knowing what you need to do, but also knowing what *not* to do in order to be successful.

Chapter 16

One of the integral parts to running an eBay business in society is learning to shift the merchandise that is to be sold to eBay buyers. When you sell merchandise, there are many things you want to take into account. One thing that was previously mentioned in a past chapter is the cost of the shipping. Since the cost of the shipping can be a major part of the cost of the entire price, which the buyer will be paying you, you want to make sure that the shipping can be as cheap as possible. This way, potential bidders will not get discouraged by a high shipping cost and will bid on your items. Also, if a bidder considers purchasing more then one item from you, if the shipping is cheap enough, they will not mind buying more items or merchandise from you because the shipping will not add up to be a great expense. You see, keeping the shipping costs low helps not just from an economical point of view of the seller's, it also encourages bidders to purchase your items and more of them.

Another thing to remember, is that a buyer might not actually be that concerned with the shipping cost. For instance, perhaps they are not so concerned with what the shipping will cost them compared to the total amount of the sale. The potential buyer is approaching the auction with the desire to buy merchandise on eBay. When they look at auctions, they are looking, for example, at a compact C.D. player, and they want to buy an Aiwa brand player that retails for $350. in the stores, so the buyer might set themselves a budget of $100. The $100. that they are willing to spend will include the shipping. If the shipping charge or the expense from the shipping company or your method of shipping costs $30., it will allow the potential bidder to spend up to $70. for the item. Since you make your money from the sale of the item and not from the shipping, you want to make sure that the shipping will cost as cheap as possible, this way the buyer will be willing to spend more money from their budget toward the cost of the item. So if the item has a shipping charge of only $20. instead of $30., the bidder, who is willing to spend a total of $100., will be paying you $80. instead of only $70., because $30. would have gone for shipping.

Now, in order to keep the cost of your shipping down, there are a few things you can do before you ship the item. One thing you will need to do is use packing supplies. One of the most used supplies is a simple cardboard box. There are many sizes and dimensions of cardboard boxes and the prices can range anywhere from $.50 a box all the way to $2. a box. Keeping the cost of the box down is very important because with many items you will be working with a very small margin, especially if you will become a high volume eBay seller, saving $1. a box or $1. per shipment will add up very quickly. Sometimes within a shipment, I can send out fifteen, twenty, or thirty boxes at a time. If I can save $1. off the cost of each cardboard box, I will be making an extra $20. or $30. per sale. An extra $20. or $30. per sale may not sound like a lot, but if you are doing ten auctions a week and you can save $200. to $300., which means putting that amount directly in your pocket, then you will be coming out ahead of the game. If you pass on that savings to your buyers, which I recommend, the buyer will be able to spend more money on the auction itself. You will have a happier buyer because you will have helped them save money, which will lead to repeat business with that buyer, and hopefully you will be able to do a great deal of business with him or her.

Now, here is another way to keep the cost of the shipping down, which is much overlooked, and is actually quite simple. You can approach stores and ask them if they have any boxes that they have received from shipments that they were going to throw away. Instead of throwing them away, would it be possible for them to set them aside every week and allow you to pick up the boxes at the end of the week? This way they will not have to deal with the hassle of flattening out the boxes, bundling them up and disposing them through the correct recycling method. Instead, all they have to do is set aside the boxes. If you consider how many boxes a large super market goes through on a daily basis, you will realize that setting up a relationship with the super market, a large retailer or a few smaller retailers, can save you money over the course of a year by helping you eliminate the cost of having to purchase cardboard boxes.

Another expense is all the tape you will need to seal the boxes and you will want to use professionally graded tape, which is excepted by the postal office and UPS, depending on which one you do your shipping with. You also want to make sure that you have the best quality tape. That kind of tape usually cannot be bought at just any store although you should be able to find it at a local packing store. A supplier of packing supplies would most likely have all that you need to purchase from them. When you purchase packing supplies, whether they are cardboard boxes, bubble filling, Scotch tape, labels, or any type of supply,.you should compare prices online, because there is an intense amount of competition and many providers of packing supplies who will be competing for your business.

One way to keep your costs down is if you see a cheaper price somewhere else, you could mention it to your current supplier and have them lower the price in order to keep your business. Very often, as I have mentioned, prices differed from supplier to supplier and I let them fight it out among each other to offer me a cheaper price. This way, I have been able to bring a bill from $100. to $70. simply by mentioning that another supplier has a cheaper price. Another thing you can do, which can help you with your cash flow, is to ask for credit from your supplier. The way to do this is to ask them, from the beginning, if they would allow you to pay your bill thirty days after you receive the merchandise. Some suppliers will instantly, without your asking, extend you a $100. credit and even give you sixty days to pay your bill. This way, you purchase the packing supplies, send out the merchandise—of course you have already been paid for your auction before hand—and now you have sixty days when instead of using some of the money you received from the buyer of the merchandise (in order to send it out to your supplier of packaging supplies), you could take that money and reinvest it in merchandise, and pay sixty days later with the proceeds of your next sale, purchasing your supplies. You stay ahead of the game by having extra money, money that you do not have to use to pay for your supplies, right away. There are many ways to keep your costs down and to give yourself credit in order to extend the cash that you have available for your business plus cash and credit that you save while running your business using some of that money to purchase more merchandise. The more merchandise you have, the more you can sell, and the more money you can make, and so on; with time, your business will continue to grow.

So now, the next question is, how do you ship your merchandise? There are many ways to go about shipping your merchandise. One way is to go to the postal office, ask them how much it costs to send the merchandise out, to have an estimate ready, giving it to potential bidders who ask you how much it will cost to ship the merchandise. Once you receive payment from the winning bidder, you go to the postal office, send out the box, and you move on to your next auction. Another method is to have the shipping done with UPS. There are many UPS centers, find the one closest to you, have the merchandise packed properly, include a label which UPS can give you, place the label on the box and send it out from the UPS center. Alternatively, for an additional $4., you can have UPS come to your location, whether it is to your house or business, to pick up the merchandise and deliver it for you. That is very convenient, especially if you send boxes very often, or if you just do not have the time to go to the post office or UPS, to send the packages yourself.

If you have a job where you do not have time during the day to go to an UPS center, then it might be ideal to let UPS come pick up the boxes from you. You could set up a morning or evening pickup from UPS. I believe an evening pickup time has a small additional charge, but it is worth it if you have a full time job and the only way for you to send out your merchandise is by UPS picking it up in during the evening. Would you rather not have that extra expense or not have your extra money coming in from your eBay business? I think you might agree with me that it is worth having to spend a little extra money on UPS if it enables you to make money with your eBay business, even while holding a full-or part-time job. Remember that UPS does not send out to any military bases or to P.O. Boxes. If you are going to be shipping to P.O. Boxes, you have to use the post office. You can tell the potential bidders that if you will be delivering to their P.O. Boxes, you will have to use the post office instead of UPS and there would be an extra $5. handling charge for having to go to the post office and spend the time going there when you could be running your business. If you feel that $5. is too high to the total price of the item that you are selling, then you could charge a $2. or a $3. handling fee, which is reasonable since most companies charge at least a handling fee of $4.95. As I mentioned earlier, you want to stay away from handling fees because once you have a handling fee then people might feel taken advantage of, especially when they could purchase the item somewhere else without a handling fee, maybe at a price near what you are charging. Avoid all handling fees unless you can give the bidder a very legitimate reason *why* there is a handling fee. I think anybody could understand that if you have to take time out of your busy day to go to a post office and stand in line for half an hour to mail out a package that you will only make a few dollars from, that the handling fee is appropriate. In that case, I think it would be reasonable to ask for a handling fee. When you send out your merchandise, always make sure that it is packed to the specifications of the shipper, whether it is UPS or the postal office. This way, if you run into any problems where the package is damaged during transportation, you will be able to claim the insurance.

In order to claim insurance on your item, you will have to pay for insurance at the postal office or through UPS; to get insurance, the total must be above the initial $100. of insurance that you automatically receive on the box. In order to claim insurance on the box you will have show the postal office or UPS the receipt for the cost of your goods. If you do not have a receipt, it might not be worthwhile to insure the merchandise because they simply will not pay for the merchandise that has been lost, unless you can show them a receipt for the value of the merchandise. You always want to insure it just so you have a fighting chance to recover some of the money and even if you do not have a receipt, you could show UPS or the postal office what the typical cost is, by showing them a catalog or by showing them receipts for similar merchandise. This strategy is not guaranteed to work, but it will give you a fighting chance when you do not have a receipt.

When you send out your merchandise with UPS, it will also give you the added protection of having the buyer sign for the merchandise to show people that he or she has received it and they can dispute it later if they have not received the merchandise. The postal service will not automatically ask for a signature from the receiver. Therefore, if you need to send out from the postal office, you should charge an extra $1.50 to have a guaranteed signature. This way, when the postal office delivers, they will ask for a signature from the recipient and you will be assured that the person received the merchandise and that it was the correct person. This way, the person can dispute later that someone else received their merchandise, instead of them. If through fraud, someone does pretend to be them, then you will be protect by the postal office or UPS because it is their responsibility to deliver the merchandise to the correct person as long as you have done everything to ensure that the merchandise is sent to the right person. As long as you have provided the correct address and spelling of the person's first and last name.

Shipping is a job within itself—many large eBay sellers who work spend a lot of time working on the shipping. What they do as their business grows is to go ahead and hire a full-or part-time person to help them with the shipping for their business. I know of one firm, which does up to $6,000. to $7,000. a month in business on eBay and you would be shocked to hear what their profit margin is— I will tell you now, between you and me, it is sometimes as high as 80% on the merchandise they are sending out. Do the math and you will see that they are making allot money; they could easily make up to $4,000. profit a week. They have a full-time person doing to the listings, a second person who separates the merchandise and describes what kind of merchandise they have. They have a third person taking pictures of the items and putting their pictures online. A fourth person is exclusively devoted to shipping out their merchandise. A fifth person purchases the merchandise, looking for good deals and negotiating. They even have another person who works on selling the merchandise, dealing with questions from eBay bidders, and working on selling additional merchandise to the buyers, once they have purchased merchandise.

As mentioned, you want to have a list of all of your eBay customers so you can try to sell them more merchandise in the future, similar to the merchandise that they have already bought from you. There are many options that you have when it comes to shipping. Another option I briefly mentioned is going to a Mailbox Plus center. Any of these private shipping centers work well and for a small fee above what UPS charges to ship the merchandise, they will pack up the merchandise for you and ship it out. That is a great option for somebody who is starting an eBay business and does not have the time to spend packing the merchandise, does not have the time to go and buy packing supplies and then having to spend the time learning how to use them. Which is not difficult, but it does take time out of your day to sort out the boxes, decide which is the best box to use, the best tape to use, and how to use the tape to seal the box correctly. The sellers who use these centers are saving a lot of time by simply dropping off the merchandise, paying for the cost of sending out the merchandise and never having to be concerned with it until it arrives with the buyer.

You should always consider your options when it comes to shipping and give yourself the right to take the easy way out when you need to. By the easy way out, be willing to pay someone else to do the grunt work; be willing to pay someone, whether it is a high school teen, a college student or a retiree, for some of the work. Pay them to have the merchandise shipped for you, to have the merchandise taken to the post office, or to have someone to wait for UPS to pick up the merchandise. You see, there is no reason why you cannot find someone else; there are many people who are looking for work who would be happy to make an extra $50 or $100 a week if you can give them work. Even as your business grows, you might decide to hire a part-time person or even a full-time employee to help you with out. It is wise to use the resources that you have at your disposal and always remember that there is an entire business sector set up just to help eBay sellers conduct their business.

Chapter 17

What is the best price to start an auction? Starting an auction on eBay requires many of the things that have been mentioned, including often being able to determine a price starting price. You see, what people see when they come to your auction is the opening bid. The opening bid is one of the major elements attracting potential bidders to your auction. The reason they are attracted to your auction based on the bid, is because it becomes more realistic in their mind whether they will be able to purchase that item, if it is worth purchasing and they could become enthusiastic or not, depending upon the price that they see.

Of course, if the bid is very, very low, if you start your auction at $1. a bid or even below $1. a bid, people will become very excited and they might say to themselves that they will be able to purchase the auction for a very, very cheap price. If people see an auction for an item priced at $1,000., starting at $1., they will be inclined to go ahead and purchase that item at $1. If they see $1,000. worth of merchandise being offered at the starting bid of $1., the price of the bidding can escalate very quickly because many people would be willing to bid up to $100. to purchase $1,000. worth of merchandise. You will have many people who are willing to bid that much because they will want to have this lifetime opportunity. In order to have those people wanting to bid, you have to show them a very good picture of what they are getting. Make sure that they see the high value of the merchandise that you are offering or of the service that you are offering and have a very low bid that will incline them to want to bid on your auction.

You might think that the solution is always to start the auction with a very low opening bid. The reason you do not want to do this is that if you have a very low opening bid, you will also take away some of the perceived value of the item that you are offering. If you have $1,000. worth of merchandise and you start the bidding at a dollar, some people will be turned off because they will say, "You know what? There has got to be to something wrong with this merchandise or this merchandise is not worth the value of how it is being portrayed and I do not even want it for $1., I do not want it for $10." For example, if you saw a $500. suit being offered with an opening bid of $1., you might say to yourself, "You know what? There has got to be holes in the suit, the suit must be irregular, or it must be low quality." If you do not see too many other bidders interested in that suit, you will think that other people much have come to the same conclusion and you will simply stay away from that suit, and not even bid $10. because if it is garbage you do not want for *any* price. There is a very delicate balance in discovering what the proper bid is for the item and having a low enough opening bid where people will be interested in bidding on your item, encourages bidders. At the same time having a high enough opening bid reflects to some extent the value of an item even at a huge discount so that people will see the perceived value and will want to bid on your item.

So if you have a collection of antique furniture that has a value of over $10,000, I think it would be reasonable for people to expect to buy this merchandise on eBay, at 80% discount, even a 90% discount, but they would not expect to be able to see that merchandise at $1. or $5. because then they would conclude that it is simply junk. Why would an eBay seller who has $10,000. worth of merchandise take a chance on selling it on eBay for $100., when they could go to an antique show, contact an antique dealer and get at least $1,000. for it? There would be nothing wrong, in order to be able to attract a lot of attention to your auction, to start the opening bid at $100. This way the bid is high enough that people say to themselves, "Look, you know what? If the opening bid is $100., this merchandise must have some value to it, otherwise nobody would even consider bidding for that opening price and the seller would not consider listing the item for an opening bid of $100."

One smart strategy that is worth using is setting the opening bid substantially higher because you will elicit a lot of interest from people who wonder why the merchandise is being auctioned off with such a high opening bid. They will say to themselves, "You know what? This merchandise must really have some value to it." Even if they do not purchase the merchandise directly from eBay and do not place a bid for the merchandise because the opening bid is too high. What will happen is, they will go ahead and contact you, send you an e-mail or call you up and they will try to find out why it is that you are offering that merchandise with such a high opening bid. When you explain to them that this antique furniture is worth $10,000. and has a wholesale value of at least $5,000., you could even arrange a private deal and sell them the merchandise for $3,000.-$4,000. You make your money, you let them make money if they want to sell it at the whole-sale value and if they are a collector, they could sell the merchandise for $10,000. You are giving people an opportunity as well as giving yourself one.

If you do have valuable merchandise, remember, people will judge the value of that merchandise or they will judge the actual merchandise by the price that you are looking to get for it. One way to ensure that, even if you have a low opening bid, that you will get the price you are looking for, use a reserve on your auction. I will go further into using a reserve in a future chapter, and at this point you should keep in mind that you always have the option of having a reserve on your auction if you decide to start with a very low opening bid. Remember, having a very low opening bid is good, especially when the value of the merchandise is clear, because you will have many people anxious to get it early. All those low opening bids for $1. $5., $10., or $20. are good for you because it means that the next bid will have to start at a higher price. Even if you have some people who are just looking for a real bargain, who are not really interested in the merchandise, could bid up to $100. for $1,000. worth of merchandise. It is a good situation because when the serious bidders come on board, they will have to start their bidding over $100.

If you are auctioning off merchandise, which clearly has a high value, say you are auctioning off a brand-new Hummer, which retails for $45,000. It is very clear to everyone that if it is a brand-new car, with a guarantee and is being sold by an established dealer, that the merchandise—in this case the Hummer—is worth $45,000. Therefore, if you put in an opening bid of $1., it will not take away from the perceived value. What will happen is you will have a lot of people excited about the auction, who are drawn in to bid and you will also have many serious people looking to bid on the Hummer. Even the people who bid $1. or $100. for that Hummer, once you draw them in, and get them to bid one time, if they are still interested in the Hummer, they will continue to bid all the way up to the price that they are willing to pay. You will have that many more bidders competing for the same item by having a very low opening bid that will draw in people for the item that you are auctioning.

Chapter 18

Now I will discuss the option of using a reserve on your auction. Before you can evaluate on the appropriateness of using a reserve on your auction, you must learn what a reserve is. A reserve is an option that eBay allows you to use. What the reserve does, is, it says that unless the high bidder for an auction bids a certain amount, the high bidder will not be considered the winning bidder of that auction, and the merchandise will not be sold to them and you will not have to pay a fee based on the final value of that auction. By using your reserve, you are ensuring that the merchandise does not sell below the price you want it to be sold. If you have for instance, a Hummer that you are auctioning off for $45,000., you want to make sure that the auction is not actually sold off to a bidder who is only bidding $100. or $1,000. for that Hummer.

If you have merchandise that costs you $100., you might want to make sure that the merchandise does not sell below your cost. Even if you are willing to auction off the merchandise at a loss, you might have decided the biggest loss that you are willing to take for that merchandise. Therefore, if you are only willing to take a $50. loss on merchandise you would set your reserve for $50. That is an advantage on using a reserve. The problem with a reserve is that it will discourage many bidders from coming into the auction. If they do not know what the reserve is, they might assume that the reserve is a lot higher then it actually is, and they will not bother bidding because no matter what, they will not be able to purchase that auction for the price that they are willing to pay.

If they see you auctioning off an expensive Persian rug, which retails for $500., and the most they are willing to bid is $200., and they see a reserve, they might say to them selves, "You know what? The reserve is probably around $500., and since I will not be able to win it because I am only willing to bid $200., then I am not going to bother to bid on the auction." On the other hand, if the reserve is not there, then that person who might be willing to bid more then what your reserve is, will bid on the auction. One strategy that eBay sellers take to circumvent this obstacle is to list in the auction description what the reserve is. They will write, "My reserve price is $300. for this $500. Persian rug." This way, bidders who are considering bidding on the auction know what the reserve is and they can decide for themselves—"Will my bid be higher then the auction, am I that interested in the auction, or will my reserve be less and I am really not that interested in the auction?" You need to decide from the beginning what is more important for you. Is it more important for you to auction off this item for the exact price that you are looking for and use a reserve, but still discourage some of the potential bidders? Or do you want to go ahead and not use your reserve and take a chance that the bidding might come in for a little less then you actually wanted it to come in for? Nevertheless, you will also have the opportunity of attracting more bidders and hopefully selling the merchandise for a much higher price then you could have, otherwise.

I would recommend when writing a good auction description, taking a decent digital picture, and having good merchandise to sell, that you do not use your reserve. If you have something of value that would cost people a lot more to purchase off-line or even from other eBay sellers, then I would not recommend using a reserve so people will be encouraged to bid on your auction. A lot of the bargain bidders will be coming in at the beginning, setting a level price for the auction and then you will have many other eBay bidders coming in at higher prices; they will be competing with each other and they will not become discouraged because of a reserve price. Unless you need to use a reserve price because you are auctioning an item that is so expensive that you cannot take a chance on a loss or you just need to make sure that you will be able to make a profit no matter what, then you need to make sure to use a reserve.

Chapter 19

Learning how to increase the profits from your auction, when the auction is completed, is extremely important for a successful eBay business. The firm that I mentioned that was making an average of $6,000. a week auctioning off on eBay makes an additional $2,000. to $3,000. by using this following method: When the auction is done, they contact a list of the highest bidders, the two or three top bidders and offer to sell them the same merchandise that they have, if they have additional units of it, at their bid. They will first try to offer the merchandise at the highest bid, and if the person does not want it at the highest bid, then they will offer it to them at the next highest bid that the second and third and fourth highest bidders were willing to pay. When they contact those people, many times, some of those high bidders, since they placed a bid on the merchandise in the first place—and they placed a pretty high bid because their bid was the second—the third in the running for the auction, they might be willing to purchase the merchandise the second time around.

Another option to make more money when the auction is over, is by contacting all the people who sent you an e-mail and all of the bidders and offer them similar types of merchandise to what they had bid on. This way, even if you do not have an additional copy of the same merchandise that they bid on in the first place, at the price that you sold the merchandise for, you can go ahead and offer them other merchandise that is complimentary. So, for instance, I put up an auction for a comic book from 1960 and it is a Superman No. 241. I only have one copy of it, but when the auction is over, I can contact the other top bidders because I know they are also interested in Superman comic books from the 1960s. I can offer each one of them another Superman comic book from the 1960s and hopefully since they placed a bid for the item in the first place, they will also be interested in having a slightly different comic book from that same era, featuring Superman. This strategy is almost guaranteed to work as long as the comic book that you are offering was not special by itself. To mean special, that there was not any reason why a buyer specifically wanted one comic book as opposed to another.

Say you are offering a music tape, featuring the greatest hits of Guns N' Roses. Even if you only have one tape featuring the greatest hits of Guns N' Roses, you might have another Guns N' Roses *album* that you could offer the second highest bidder and you might happen to have another Guns N' Roses album that you could offer the third highest bidder; so you could make more money from the same auction. The key is when you have an auction, set up an auction for an item in which you have additional units, so that you could always try to sell more units to the second, third, and fourth highest bidders.

You want to have more units, so you can give the option to the highest bidder to buy more of the same. You also want to have similar units before the auction starts so you can offer the similar units to the second, third, and fourth highest bidder and you can also offer the highest bidder similar units of what they have bid on. You see, if the highest bidder bought that Superman comic book from the 1960s, then chances are that they will want other Superman comic books from the 1960s. There have been instances where buyers have purchased a lot of comic books from me and they said that they would really like the option to purchase other lots, right now, of some more comic books. I ended up sending them two or three lots of comic books, instead of just that one lot. What I could do is offer to the highest bidder another type of comic book or another lot that is similar to what it is they are purchasing. It is to your advantage to have similar merchandise to be able to offer to the highest bidder and the other bidders who bid on your auction, and also to have other types of merchandise that is complementary to the highest bidders so they will have the option of purchasing your merchandise. There are many ways to make money when the auction is completed.

Another way to make money is to ask the high bidder questions as to what type of merchandise they are interested in. Aside from what they bought from you, they might have other interests and needs. Somebody who bought a Superman comic book from me from the 1960s might also be interested in non-fiction books from the 1960s. They might be interested in records and you know what? They might have other interests that have nothing to do with comic books at all! They might be looking for a brand-new sofa for their living room and if I can locate a brand-new sofa for their living room, I can make an additional profit by selling them a sofa.

You want to ask as many questions as possible from your high bidders to find out what other kind of merchandise they are looking for and what other services they can use. Therefore, if you are doing a service auction, then you also want to know what other kind of services they can use and what they could utilize for their auction. One other method for making money after the auction is over does not come directly from selling to the highest bidders, it is the way you make money; ask them if they have any merchandise that they no longer use or no longer want to have and you buy it from them. The collector or the dealer who purchased the Superman comic book from the 1960s, might have other comic books that he or she is no longer interested in having and might be willing to sell them at a good price because they want to spend their money on other comic books. I take those other comic books from the 1960s, and I sell them to the other highest bidders or I sell them to future bidders through future auctions. Alternatively, at this point, if you already have a list of 50 or sixty people who have purchased items or books or computers or C.D.s from your auctions, you can take the new merchandise that you bought from this high bidder, and sell it to your list of other bidders. Again, there are many ways for you to make money from your auctions as long as you are creative and you consider all of your auctions.

Remember, every buyer is also a source of merchandise and every source of merchandise is also a source of sales. By that I mean, suppose you have a source where you buy your socks from, and you know what? This person you buy your socks from, they also sell underwear and t-shirts, and the only thing you are interested in buying from them is socks because that is what your business is; it is selling socks on eBay. What you can do is, when you find a really good deal on men's underwear or women's underwear, you could go ahead and purchase the underwear at a really good price, contact your supplier of socks and offer the underwear that you bought at a very, very reduced price to the supplier. If this person has bought merchandise from you in the past, has sold you merchandise through eBay, you have an option or opportunity to continue to make money once your auction is done. Remember that in every auction, offer people consulting services. If somebody is a comic book collector, offer to help them find other comic books or to help with the comic book business on eBay or off eBay, for a fee. You could market your expertise—and your expertise is proven once you have interacted with a buyer or seller on eBay. You always have an option to enhance your revenues by offering your services on eBay and you could also offer unrelated services and consulting on eBay. You could list, in your "About You" page or on your store on eBay—eBay allows you to set up a store where you can sell your merchandise or your services directly—a list on that eBay page or in the eBay store; of all the other types of services and products that you offer. You could add in your auction description that you have other types of services that you could offer that seller or buyer, whichever the case may be.

Chapter 20

If you have spent any time going to thrift shops or small clothing stores, you are familiar with the term consignment sales. Consignment sales is a process where the owner of the merchandise gives merchandise to a seller and the seller sells the merchandise for them. Once the sale is completed the seller of the merchandise keeps a commission and gives the rest of the proceeds of the sale to the past owner. This provides a benefit to both the owner and seller. The owner of the merchandise now has an outlet, which will be working on selling his or her merchandise. They do not have to concern themselves with paying for the merchandise, paying for the advertising, locating buyers, meeting with the buyers, showing the merchandise, researching the market, and worrying about collecting payment for the merchandise.

In a consignment sale, the seller gains because they do not have to risk any money investing in inventory. The seller does not have to go ahead and purchase merchandise which might not sell well or perhaps not sell for as much money as the seller intended it to. Say the merchandise seller has a $200. VCR. If the seller had to go to the wholesaler and spend $100. to buy the VCR and then the merchandise never sold, then the seller would be out $100. If, on the other hand, the seller never had to buy that merchandise for $100. in the first place, you know what? Any money they made on it would become profit, even if it did not sell for as high as the seller thought it would sell. If it does not sell at all, the seller could always return it to the owner, or whoever gave them the VCR, but chances are, the person who owns the VCR is not going to want to take it back because they already gave it to the seller and has no other way of selling it. Therefore, the seller can actually keep the merchandise for as long as they need to, until they can sell it.

If the merchandise sells for less then the seller thought it was going to sell for, it is not a problem because the seller still makes some money since they are collecting a percentage of the revenue that came in from the sale of the VCR.

Usually, this type of activity comes when the owner of the merchandise is having a very difficult time selling the merchandise and is willing to give up proceeds and take a chance of not receiving the amount of money that they wanted to receive. The owner of the merchandise might feel that they will not make any money on it at all and it would just sit in their warehouse for months, if not years. Now as an eBay seller, you can take advantage of this great business method by contacting owners of slow-moving merchandise and offering to sell it for them on a consignment basis. When you sell it on consignment, you set up an agreement where you can keep anywhere form 5%-50% of the proceeds from the sale of the merchandise.

Consignment sales work very well with clothing, electronics, or any merchandise that can be properly auctioned off. In order to set up a solid consignment sale with someone, you need to make sure that you have a good relationship, let them know that you are trustworthy, and that you perceive yourself as a professional. The person giving you the merchandise should be glad to give you the merchandise as long as you are going to attempt to sell it and as long as he or she feels that you will do a good job of selling the merchandise. They will not give you the merchandise just for you to simply hold on to it and they definitely will not give you the merchandise if they feel that you might lose, damage, or at the worst, steal the merchandise. You always want to make sure to portray yourself a professional if you want to be a successful consignment seller. You want to be able to show people that you have a track record of running successful consignment sales.

If you have never run a consignment sale before and you would need to have at least one consignment sale to attract more people to your consignment sales, then you might try the following strategy. You can take the merchandise from the owner, agree to sell it and keep a very low percentage—this way the incentive for the owner is that once the sale is completed, he or she will still be receiving a majority of the proceeds, as much as 95%. Why would you want to do this, basically give away all your profits? Because if you start out small with that owner of the merchandise, they will most likely entrust you with more merchandise in the future, and then you could go ahead and sell it at a decent profit. Sometimes it is worthwhile making a small profit or not even making a profit at the beginning, in hopes of capturing a steady stream of larger profits in the future. When you do a consignment sale, you have another option that is very good if you do not have a lot of storage space. You could make an agreement to have the owner of the merchandise to store the merchandise at his or her location if you agree to pick up the merchandise once the sale is done. The owner of the merchandise will most likely be comfortable with this arrangement because they will not have to worry about theft, loss, or any accidents taking place because he or she is still in control of the merchandise since they have possession of it.

You could take this a step further and offer this arrangement to the owner of the merchandise by telling the owner you would like to do the packing and the shipping from the location. You could even pay to have him or her pack up the merchandise and you could reimburse them for the cost of the shipping. The actual shipping cost will be paid by the buyer, so you could reimburse them for the cost of having the merchandise packed and the time packing and setting the merchandise up so it can be picked up by UPS or the cost of taking it to the post office. You would bill in that cost with the sale while the auction takes place. If it is worthwhile to give up some of the profits in order save the hassle of having to pack and ship out the supplies, you could also offer to make a compromise. By telling the owner of the merchandise that you will only take 30% or 35% if they agree to pack up the merchandise and have it ready for UPS or pack it and take it to UPS, you are offering to forgo your usual fee of 40% of the proceeds of the sale. Remember, the buyer will always be paying for the cost of shipping; otherwise the owner of the merchandise will not want to deal, because they simply will not make any money if they have to give up both the time it will take them to pack up the merchandise, the cost of the merchandise, and sending it out.

So who can you conduct a consignment arrangement with? You could walk into a store in your local neighborhood, such as a clothing store and say, "Hey look, you're now approaching winter and you still have some summer overstock left over. Why don't you let me sell your summer overstock? I could sell it to places around the country where they still need summer clothing and instead of you having to mark down your inventory by 50% or more, I will sell the clothing for as close to the retail price as possible, and I would like 25% of the proceeds." The owner of the store gains, because instead of having to mark down the merchandise by 50%, losing 50% of the retail value, they will only be losing 25% or 30% of the retail value, because you will only be taking 25% or 30% as your part of the sale. Now, to be fair to the owner of the clothing store, based on your past studies, what price the merchandise actually goes for, you base the price of the clothing on that knowledge. You want to make sure that everything is stated up front and, in order to encourage the owner of the merchandise to want to be an active participant in this consignment arrangement, go ahead and show them what similar merchandise has been sold for, in the past.

Personally, I would not divulge my sales outlets. I would not let the owner of the merchandise know that you will be selling the merchandise on eBay unless there is a specific restriction on selling the merchandise on eBay. Otherwise you do not need to provide this information on eBay, since you might encourage the owner of the merchandise to try to sell the merchandise the same way that you will be selling it. The only thing that you should let the owner of the merchandise know, is that you have an arrangement through which you could sell merchandise throughout the country at a decent price as long as you could charge below the retail price. This way, someone who otherwise might have taken a loss on the merchandise will now be able to recoup their initial investment, and even be able to make a profit when you take into account the cost of the merchandise and your fee, which you will be taking for conducting the sale.

You could also set up a consignment sale with a bookseller; sell their overstock, the books that are not moving. With a ninety-nine cent store that has merchandise they bought that is not selling well in their area, you could contact wholesalers, liquidators, close-out brokers, and manufacturers and set up arrangements with them to help them with their sales. When you have a consignment arrangement set up, always make sure to put it in writing. If you do not have it in writing, you are going to find it very difficult to continue the relationship, especially if the merchandise is in the possession of the owner. It is always a good idea to protect yourself by having everything in writing. Also, even as the owner and seller of the merchandise, you might want to consign out to another seller and have them move your merchandise. Having everything in writing so there are no disputes, becomes the easiest way to resolve any of these situations by consulting the written agreement, in any given situation. Consignment sales are a great way to make money and I highly recommend it for eBay sellers who are not interested in purchasing inventory. Imagine, what could be better than running a business where your only cost is the advertising fee, which on eBay is simply the listing fee, which is quite small for most auctions.

Chapter 21

In business, there are many opportunities to buy good quality merchandise at very good prices. Many businesses baulk at the opportunity to buy the merchandise only because they are unsure how the merchandise will fair in their market, even though the merchandise might look very good and they might be able to get it at a very good price and make a good profit with it. The reason they are not sure whether they should buy it or not is there is always a chance in any given market they will not be able to sell the merchandise. So they want to be careful before they buy, and wouldn't life be simpler if they had a crystal ball to forecast the future, knowing if it is worthwhile or not. They could have their money invested in the merchandise that they know will sell well, however the reason the business will not take a chance on all types of merchandise, even when they can get it at a very good deal, is because if the merchandise does not end up selling very well, they would not make a substantial profit. To be sure, one of the biggest fears for businesses is buying merchandise that will not sell at all where they are not able to recoup their investment, or half of their investment, and they could end up having to take a total loss. As an owner of a small business, whether you have an eBay, retail, or a wholesale business, you want to be careful with the inventory you buy, because any money you tie into your merchandise, will naturally, be your own money.

As you know today, money is not easy to come by and you want your business to grow, so you might want to be as careful as you can in purchasing only good quality merchandise. So how do you ensure to purchase only good quality merchandise? The best way is to test out the merchandise, first. If you have a small retail store, you could take a few samples, put them on display, and see how customer's react. The challenge with that is if you take a few pieces of merchandise and put them in a store or if a wholesaler shows a few pieces of merchandise to a few of their customers, it is still not the best way to get a good reading on whether the merchandise will sell or not. The reason is because the merchandise you are looking to sell has to have a wide-appeal. If you go to one or two stores and put the merchandise on the counter, even if some people react positively to that merchandise, there is no way to tell what the general consensus will be for that merchandise and you cannot live off of one or two customers. Therefore, it is wise to make sure that there is a wide-appeal for that merchandise.

On the other hand, say nobody is interested in the merchandise, say you displayed a few pieces of units of what you purchased, because you got a great deal on pens and you have a thousand pens for sale. Now, you only have five or six pens up for auction, so you put these pens up for sale and add a few for sale on the counter in the store and not one single customer wants them. Say you are a wholesaler and not one single store, or any of your retail accounts is interested in those pens. That is still not a good gauge as far as whether the pens are a good product, because you have only gone to a very small, limited number of potential customers. If you sell to the larger public, you would get a good reading. However, if you are a wholesaler it is hard to go to a good number of customers because you have a very limited amount of time and you are still dealing with your normal products and your regular business, thus your time is tied up and restricted.

The eBay site takes the whole situation and turns it upside down because what it allows you to take one sample of the item you want to sell and put it up on an auction for sale; this way you can see how many visitors your auction receives, and how many people checked it out. The eBay site allows you to put a counter your auction page for free, and that counter will keep track of all the hits the auction receives. So when you describe what you are selling clearly in your headline, people come to your auction because they are interested in that particular item that you have for sale. In the case where you have the opportunity to buy a thousand pens at a few pennies a pen, that will not add up to much money; with the opportunity to buy 50,000. pens, that can be a money maker. I once saw 50,000. quality pens sell for about two cents a pen—now *that* is a great opportunity because a pen can retail at a $.99 store for one dollar each or two for a dollar. You would have a great opportunity to make money in the purchase of those pens!

When you go on eBay, you need to create a clear headline of what it is that you have for sale. You see how many people come to visit your auction page and you know how many people are interested in buying those pens. Of course, you do not want to sell one pen at a time, so say you sell the pens in groups of 100 or 50, this way students, office managers, small businesses, wholesalers, and retailers could all potentially be ideal customers. If you see that you begin the auction and you get 400 or 500 hits to your site, then you know that you have a very good product that people are interested in. Even if you receive only 100 or 200 visitors, that is a good start because you know that there is an interest in the pens. You also might want to look at how many bidders you receive, what the highest bid is for, and what people are willing to bid for the pens.

To take this a step further, you might decide to sell the entire group of pens that you buy—say you put up an auction for 50,000 pens and see what the highest bid is. If the highest bid is $1,000. for 50,000 pens, which comes out to about $.02 a pen, just make sure to buy the pens for under $0.02 and you have a guaranteed profit. Since you already have a high bidder willing to pay $.02 a pen, and you already know that they are going to take 50,000 pens and even better, if you can wait and receive the money from them beforehand, then go ahead and act on the deal, buy the pens, sell them and make a good profit. What if instead of selling the 50,000 pens for $.02 each, what if you ended up selling them for $.05 or $.06 each? That would be a really good amount of money. You could even attempt to sell 10,000, so once you know how those pens sell, you can make a decision on buying an entire lot of 50,000 pens and then continue selling the rest of pens in lots of 10,000. A small store or even a wholesaler, using the standard business method that they practice, does not have the opportunity to gage instantly or in three to seven days what the demand is, for a certain product. How can you know how many products will sell and how much money they will pay for the product, knowing how much money they will be getting for the product? However, with your eBay business, you can instantly know how much money you will be making by selling the merchandise, how much you want to pay for the merchandise and if there is a demand for your merchandise.

Say in the situation where you buy the 50,000 pens that you test out on eBay, you know that there is a given market for those pens, and then you do not even have to try to sell on eBay all of the 50,000 pens at once. What you can do, is out of those 50,000 pens, you take 500 pens and you auction them off on eBay before you actually go ahead and purchase the pens. That way, you can find out if there is a demand for the 500 pens. You can see for yourself what price people are willing to pay for the 500 pens, based on the number of hits that the auction received, the number of bids, the highest bid, and what the bids were from the top three or four bidders. You can see if there is a good demand for the pens and if it is worthwhile to buy the pens because even if you spend six months selling 50,000 pens, you know by having an auction for 500 pens each and every three or five days, that it does not matter if the profit is worthwhile. Say you sell 500 pens for $50., so you have made $.10 a pen. If you buy those pens for a penny each, your total cost will for the pens will be $500., right? At $.10 a pen, that would be $5,000. and $.01 a pen would be $500. Now say you average selling those pens for $.10 each or more conservatively, for $.05 each and it takes you three months to sell all the pens. At $.05 each, you have 50,000 pens; $.10 a pen would give you $5,000., $.05 a pen would give you $2,500., and your profit on the pens is $2,500. Therefore, it is definitely worth going in on that transaction, but if you did not know what the proceeds could be for that auction, you would be very hesitant to buy the pens. I would not recommend spending $500., just because you want to take a chance and because you believe that the pens might sell well.

As you can see, eBay allows you to go in, without having to be blind and you gives you an educated guess beforehand and I would even call it more than an educated guess, because you will know whether you can afford to buy the merchandise or not. There are many situations where you can use eBay to take a lot of the guesswork out of the business. Reverting to the previous example, when I said the pens will cost you $500. and your profit is $2,500., or perhaps $2,000., that might not sound like a great deal of money—keep in mind that hopefully it is not the only product you are selling on eBay. If over the course of three months you had ten similar transactions, each transaction giving you an average profit of $2,000., or $20,000. in three months, divide that in thirds and you are talking about almost $7,000. of profits per *month*. So you can see, there will be many times, even if one transaction might not seem to yield such a vast profit, where as long as you keep moving and listing auctions on eBay, the profits will add up.

I once bought a truck load worth of merchandise because I had investigated what the market would be for those items. Even though, as I mentioned with the example of the pens, it took me a few months to sell the merchandise, I was confident that once I would sell it, I would be sitting on a decent profit. The truck load of merchandise was only one of the many items that I was selling on eBay. As long as you test out the products that you will be selling, you will be a ahead in the process of eliminating the risk of holding on to merchandise that does not sell well or does not sell, period. The key point that you can see from this chapter is to test out the demand of the product before you actually purchase it. Additionally, when you have an opportunity to invest a lot of money in merchandise, do not hesitate, do not be worried that you are spending a great deal of money as long as you have taken various factors into consideration, including testing out the market and seeing if there is a demand for the item(s).

Chapter 22

One of the big controversies on eBay is whether sellers should sell to international bidders. International bidders, such as bidders from Canada, who are not a big issue, they are mostly referring to the problem of selling to international bidders due to the high frequency of fraud that eBay sellers experience after they receive payment and send out the merchandise. The dilemma is that once the merchandise is sent out, there is no way to bring the merchandise back and if the buyer is based overseas, it would be very hard to pursue any legal recourse to recover the merchandise. One of the problems with international bidders is that there are many instances where fraud is involved with credit card payments. Many bidders will buy an item with a stolen credit card and have it shipped internationally, disputing the charge afterward, similar to what can be done in the United States. If someone disputes a charge here in the states, there is legal recourse; and steps you can take to recover the merchandise. If the same situation takes place overseas, you might never be able to find the person again and you would have to go through an entire legal system that you are not familiar with, plus the legal costs could easily be thousands of dollars while working overseas and you are simply out of your merchandise.

So how can you go ahead and conduct business with international bidders? There are ways you can do it. Before you decide if you do want to deal with international bidders, keep in mind the high cost of shipping the merchandise that you will be sending out. That might discourage many bidders who are based overseas. What you do not want to happen, after the auction is completed and the international bidder sees how much is shipping is going to cost them, is for them to decide not to complete the auction. You will be out of the time that you spent listing the auction and waiting for the auction to end, and you will have to re-list the item again, losing the listing fee to eBay. You will also lose the money it will cost you, to list the merchandise a second time. As you can see, there are many considerations you have to take into account.

In order to address the first concern, about the high cost of shipping, let the international bidders know, right upfront how much shipping will cost. Let them know that they must contact you as soon as they place their bid or before they place a bid; that would be ideal, in regards to the cost of the shipping. You can tell them that the only way an international bidder can bid on your auction is if they received a call from you for the cost of the shipping and if on top of that quote, the bidder has acknowledged receiving the shipping quote. Also, make it very clear to international bidders that the only form of payment you will accept will be from a money order that you recognize, from a legitimate bank, or from American Express, Western Union or Money Gram, or another form of accepted payment. Let the international bidder know that if they send you a personal check, you will have to hold it for a minimum of three weeks, to make sure that it clears and even three weeks in many situations might not be enough.

I have heard of a situation where after two months of someone receiving and cashing a check, the bank discovered that it was a fraudulent check and the funds were removed from that person's bank account. Dealing with international bidders can be a precarious situation because if you do not do it correctly, you could be out on the listing fees and merchandise that you sent out to the winning bidder. On the other hand, it can be very lucrative, because if it is done properly, you will increase your marketplace to all of the eBay members who are located in Canada and overseas. Think about how many more millions and millions of potential customers you will have by being able to sell merchandise, not to only to the eBay members in the United States, but also to the eBay members in Canada, France, Poland, Hungary, Israel, China, and Japan. You are opening up a market of 100,000,000 people, at least, of people who have access to a computer and can bid on eBay. The eBay site has 60,000,000 members in the U.S. alone. Think about how many more they have overseas and how many more people just browse eBay both in the United States and overseas and if they see something they like, they will become a registered user just to bid on your merchandise because they will be interested. If you have something of quality to offer on eBay and you strongly believe that there is a strong market for that merchandise overseas, then I recommend you set up a system where you can sell to international bidders so that you can capture money that they are willing to spend on eBay.

So what kind of merchandise will sell well to international bidders? Among some of the merchandise that sells very well are American brands. People overseas—and I can attest to that because I grew up in Mexico—love American brands—they love Levi's, Tommy Hilfiger, Calvin Klein, any brand that screams out, "This is an American brand!" They love any product—aside from clothing—that is American:

American music, American movies, American collectibles, they even love pictures of tourist destinations such as a painting of the Statue of Liberty. Remember, anything that says American on it or conveys the United States, will sell very well overseas. As long as you protect yourself well, you can make a great deal of money selling American-brand products.

Another item that sells well overseas is collectibles. Collectibles such as comic books, antiques, or postcards sell very well overseas. There are many items that are not in supply in other countries such as English books. People will use English books for their educational value or to brush up on their English skills. Perhaps they are setting up an English library overseas and if you go to garage sales, or to used books stores and you buy English books, then you will have a very good market overseas. A book that might only cost you $.10 or $.20 here in the United States, might be sold overseas in France, Russia, or Africa for $.30 or $.40 a book because there are many people there who would love to learn English. Perhaps they are planning on immigrating to the United States some day, and they want to be better prepared to do business and work in the United States. They want to give their children a basic understanding of the English language and they will be happy to buy anything that will teach them the language. There are many products, which I have mentioned, which can be sold very well on eBay to both international bidders and domestic bidders, however keep in mind that you need to be careful. Similar to being careful with international bidders; you need to be careful with domestic bidders, to ensure that you are protected as a seller and that you are only receiving merchandise once you are sure that the funds for the merchandise have been paid for.

Chapter 23

I want to tell you about a method that will encourage an eBay bidder who is not too sure about buying merchandise from you, to purchase from you. The fact may be that they do not know you or they are not familiar with you. Maybe you are a new eBay seller and they are not comfortable sending you money, or you could have low or negative feedback, or it could be a situation where the item that is being auctioned off on eBay is a very expensive item. Suppose a buyer might not feel comfortable sending off $1,000. or more, for merchandise that they have not purchased before, from a seller who they do not know.

How do you solve this problem? You see, the problem is, most likely, more of a trust issue then a financial problem. The person is willing to spend the money; they have committed themselves to purchasing the auction from you, but suddenly they are reluctant because they have not dealt with you, before. The problem could even arise where the person does not want to place a bid in the first place because they want to see how high the price of the auction is going. They might not feel comfortable committing themselves to sending money to someone who they are not familiar with and they might buy the merchandise, receive it, only to discover it is not what has been described. Imagine spending $1,000. on a piano, the piano arrives and it does not even work—or worse, it is not the same piano as described in the auction. Therefore, it is understandable why people would be hesitant to send money to someone who they have never dealt with before and even if they *have* dealt with the person before, they may be spending a great deal of money, in this transaction and feel uncomfortable about it. The best method for calming people's fears and to help make people more comfortable to send you money is by letting people in the auction know that they can use an escrow service. An escrow service is a third party that will hold the funds until the buyer has received the merchandise and approved the merchandise.

The way an escrow would work is, if Larry purchases a used piano on eBay from Frank, Larry would send the funds to an escrow service, and the escrow service would confirm with Frank that they have received the funds. They would let Frank know how much money they have received, how they have received the money and if the funds have cleared. Once the funds have been cleared, then Frank would send out the merchandise, in this case the used piano, to Larry. Larry would then let the escrow service know that he is happy with the used piano that he has received. The escrow service would release the funds to Frank, who sold the piano. However, while an escrow service can work well, there are certain reasons, as a seller, you would not want to use the escrow service.

For instance, in this situation, Larry said, "You know what? I am really not happy with the piano. The piano did not meet my exact specifications, it is a good piano, but it is not the way is was described in the auction." He might simply be upset with his purchase for some other reason, and he tells the escrow service that the piano he received is a piece of junk. Now, the escrow service will not release the money to Frank because Frank has already sent out the piano. He is out of his merchandise, spent his money listing the piano, paid for the shipping because he has not received the money or was reimbursed for the shipping yet and Frank is now in a very tough situation. The buyer in this situation might call you up and say, "Look, the money is in an escrow service and I really do not need this merchandise, I do not even want the merchandise at this point." He could tell you straight out that he is going to refuse to accept the merchandise unless you offer him a better deal. Even though that would be unscrupulous on the buyer's part, there are buyers who do that. Why put yourself in what could be a very unfortunate situation and give the buyer the upper hand?

What I recommend to you—and you do not want to give the buyer an option to use the fact that the money is in an escrow account as leverage to extract a better deal from you, is to ask for some of the money upfront. Instead of using an escrow service, unless you have received your cost for the item upfront and then you can allow the rest of the price of the item to be sent to an escrow account you do not have to explain the breakdown to the buyer, but what you *can* tell the buyer is, "Look, I am willing to use an escrow account for this $1,000. item as long as you send me $300. or $400. upfront and the rest you could put in an escrow account." If the buyer is honest, they will understand that for $300. or $400., they are not taking such a big risk compared to the value they will be receiving, because if worst comes to worst, they will still be receiving the $1,000. piano for only $300. The fee that you are charging upfront, or the money that you want besides, will be going into an escrow account and should also cover the cost of shipping. This way, at the worst, you will not have lost any money. Even when the buyer receives the merchandise and says that he is not happy with what he has received; the most that you stand to lose is your profit on the item because the buyer will have already paid you your cost for the merchandise, plus shipping.

When is it a good time to use an escrow account? If the buyer of the merchandise is willing to travel to you and pick up the merchandise from you and you do not have to send it out, in that case, I do not see any reason why you should not use an escrow account. If someone travels to you, they are showing a serious commitment on their part. So you know that they are not looking to rip you off, or to take advantage of you and you could see that the fact that they are coming to look at the merchandise, that they do want it and are hoping that the merchandise will be good. Now, say that they come to your warehouse, or your garage and look at the merchandise and say, "You know what? This merchandise is not what I thought it would be!" This is not a problem—they do not have to take their merchandise with them, you call up the escrow account and the escrow account will simply return their money to them. Make it very clear in the auction description that even if the money is in an escrow account, just because they are not happy with the merchandise, it does not mean the escrow account could just give them their money back.

The only time the escrow service will give them their money back, and you should set up an agreement that will stipulate this clearly, is if the merchandise is not described as according to the way that it is. Not by saying that it is red and it is really fire engine red, while instead, it is dragon red. You want it to be a situation, first of all, where the merchandise is considered to be described properly. Where you might call it red, maybe it was the color yellow; even a dark orange color—that is not a good enough reason to let the sale fall through. Someone will always be interested in your item and as long as they are a serious bidder, and you have not misrepresented the item on purpose, as long as the tone of the color or the actual color has not changed the value of the item, then the buyer should be satisfied with the merchandise that is being offered. Using an escrow account can be a good idea, because it will help you solicit bids from bidders who would otherwise not have bid and also allow bidders to feel more comfortable so that they will end up bidding a good deal more for the merchandise than they had originally planned and you will make more money.

Another good reason to use an escrow service is when you are selling an item, that you mentioned will be picked up, but also an item that does not need to be delivered, such as when you are providing a service. Now, with a service you have to be careful because you do not want them to dispute that you have not provided the service. What you can do is receive the money, put it in an escrow account and agree that once you commence the service that you will be providing, the money needs to be transferred from the escrow account to you. This way, the buyer of the service will be able to see that you are serious, that you are providing the service that you said you would be providing and at that point, will feel comfortable knowing that they have paid you for your service.

An additional reason to use an escrow service is when you sell a business. If you sell a business and the person wants to know that you have portrayed the business the way that it is and the business is producing the revenues or profits that you claim that it is producing, you want to allow that bidder to use an escrow service. That way, the bidder knows that you are not trying to misrepresent anything because if you did, they could take their money back. Even in a situation where someone bought the business, and they turned out to be a fraudulent buyer, then they requested their money back even though the business was actually performing the way it was performing, you have not lost much because you could take back possession of the business. If they renege on the deal, you have lost out on the listing fee and your time, but it is not the end of the world. You could easily go ahead and take possession of the business again and sell it to another bidder. An escrow account allows you both as a buyer and seller to protect yourself and also opens up opportunities to make more money as long as you realize what the downside is to accepting an escrow account.

Chapter 24

Setting up a return policy for your business is important. Like any type of business, where there is a buyer and seller, the buyer of the merchandise or the service wants to have some sort of guarantee that they will be receiving what it is that is being offered. If you want to take this principle and apply it to the fullest extent, you offer a full thirty-day guarantee return policy on the merchandise being offered. By law, anytime someone purchases something by mail, there has to be a return policy.

Now what you can do on eBay, since eBay is an auction, is set up an as-is final auction where the person has the right to come inspect the merchandise. That way there will be no problem with disputing the merchandise later. The reason there is no problem is because the person buying the merchandise had every right to come in beforehand, inspect the merchandise and make sure that the merchandise met their specifications and the buyer knows what it is that they are receiving. You see, even making it as an as-is auction, a final auction is setting up a return policy, that is also *your* return policy. Simply, there are no returns and you are giving the person the right to come in and inspect the merchandise. If you are selling an item in which you do not mind if it is returned, such as a VCR or a TV, as long as it is in the original packaging and it has not been opened, then it is okay, period. Specifically in that situation, you could offer a return policy that will encourage bidders to bid on your item and spend more money on the item because they know that if the item is not what it was portrayed to be, they have the option of returning it.

The downside of allowing people to return merchandise is that they can damage the merchandise that they purchased from you. They could use up the merchandise or even send you similar merchandise, and not the same quality. That happens in many instances with comic books—that is why I do not allow people to return merchandise with comic books. I allow them to inspect the merchandise, check it out, and decide for themselves whether the merchandise meets their specifications and only *then* do I suggest they bid on the merchandise. They do not have to come inspect it if they feel comfortable based on my feedback, the photographs, the auction description, and they need to realize that once they purchase the merchandise they will not be able to return it.

As you see what happens with comic books, say someone buys a very high-grade comic book or they have just purchased a baseball card in mint condition. Now that baseball card is a rare card and especially in such mint condition. They buy the card and they are very happy. You know what they do once they receive the card? They call you up and say they are not really happy with the condition of the card, send it back to you and you say that is fine, okay, send the card back to you will refund their money. When you receive the baseball card you notice that they have not sent the same baseball card back. What they did is they purchased the same baseball card or they might have already had the same baseball card in their collection, but in poor condition. They then send that baseball card to back, you have to refund them their money, they keep the mint baseball card, and now you are sitting with a worthless baseball card or a baseball card that is worth a lot less money because it is not in mint condition. Now, there are a very, very small number of people who will ever engage in that type of fraud. Nevertheless, you still want to protect yourself because your profit margin might be very small and if you are taken advantage of during one auction, it might take you many more auctions before you recoup your loss from that auction. So to be very honest and clear, I suggest to always tell people that they are more then welcome to come inspect the merchandise, even come pick up the merchandise themselves, after the auction is completed, and then all sales are final. So why do you allow people to come pick up the merchandise themselves? Because they know that if they are going to meet the seller face-to-face and if they are going to be picking up the merchandise from the seller directly, the seller would not engage in any fraud because they will have to face the buyer when they come to pick up the merchandise. So make sure that you have a solid return policy that will not hurt your business, and make sure that at the same time your return policy is fair and encourages bidders to bid and buy at your auction.

Chapter 25

Aside from selling to bidders on eBay, there is another way to make money. The other way to make money on eBay is not only focus on the eBay buyers, also focus on the eBay sellers. There are many opportunities to make money by selling to people who are looking to set up business on eBay. There are many methods and I will analyze a few of them, step by step. The first way to do it is, as mentioned throughout the book, is by having auctions set up where you are providing information in your consulting services for other people who want to sell on eBay. The way you do that is by having auctions set up specifically where you list your expertise, what you have sold on eBay, what you know about selling on eBay, and what it is that you are looking to help people sell. If you have been able to successfully sell merchandise such as furniture, you could use that expertise to help people sell their merchandise on eBay, more specifically furniture. You could also make it clear to people that aside from knowing how to sell furniture, you can apply the same skills that you developed while selling furniture to help them sell their own merchandise.

Another way to sell to eBay sellers is by showing them ways to sell without having to give the information, or to get into your consulting advice. What do I mean by that? You can write books, such as the book I have now produced, or other books that they have on eBay to help teach people how to sell on eBay. I have seen many books on eBay by different authors and some of them are pretty helpful, showing people how to make money by selling various items on eBay. People need information, just like people need books on how to invest, how to garden, how to cook, how to have better relationships. People also need and enjoy reading books on prospering in their eBay business. So to benefit from your eBay business, you need to have information that people will be willing to buy in order to prosper in their own business on eBay.

One method of making money by selling to eBay sellers is by selling packing supplies to eBay sellers. Every eBay seller who is selling merchandise that needs to be shipped, is in need of packing supplies. If you can obtain packing supplies at a very good price or even obtain the packing supplies for free, as was mentioned getting them from supermarkets or stores who no longer need the boxes, you can turn around and sell this merchandise to sellers. You could make yourself a good profit if you are getting the merchandise for free, 100% of the sale is profit, and even if you have to pay for the merchandise and get the merchandise for a very good price, you could walk away with at least a 50% profit margin. Look at it another way, you are making a 100% markup on the merchandise that you are selling and that merchandise is packing supplies. How else can you make money by selling to eBay sellers? If you buy a large lot of merchandise, you could turn around and sell that merchandise to other eBay sellers with the intention of allowing them to resell the merchandise.

So, for example, say you found a case of 100 pairs of sneakers. Now, these sneakers are brand-new Nike sneakers, which retail for $95. at the store and you buy them for $25. a pair. You might have gone to an auction or you might have bought them from a store that is going out of business. You have now 100 pairs of sneakers, all in their original boxes. You could turn around and sell them to eBay sellers who are in the business of reselling merchandise and, specifically, eBay sellers who sell sneakers. Tell them you will offer the $95. retail sneakers for $60. or $65. a pair. They still can make a decent amount of money, even if they offer the brand-new sneakers at a $10. or $15. discount, compared to the full retail price, and since you only paid $25. a pair, you can make a $40. profit per pair. If you sell 100 pairs to the resellers, then you would be making $4,000. on the entire lot. Let us say you want to sell them very quickly so you can mark up the sneakers by $10. or $15. compared to what you paid for them and you will still be making a good deal amount of money while allowing people who are in the business of selling on eBay to make a good amount of money, also. It's a win-win situation. Remember, that you are not just making money from the first sale you are also making money from the future sales that you will make to eBay resellers or eBay sellers.

Once you develop a relationship with them they will know that you are a good source for quality merchandise at a very good price. There are many ways to make money by selling merchandise on eBay at a very good price when you gear that merchandise to eBay sellers. You can then make it your business to contact auctioneers, liquidators and look for merchandise that eBay sellers would be interested in selling. How can you figure out what merchandise eBay sellers would be interested in selling? You look at the auctions that are taking place, and you see what merchandise is generally being sold is and what sold the most. That way you know which merchandise sells well, and that eBay sellers who sell it are succeeding with that merchandise. You know that if they are succeeding with that merchandise they will need more of it. You could contact the eBay sellers before you purchase the merchandise and offer it to them. Tell them what price that you have it available for and then you can see whether they would be interested in buying this merchandise from you at the price that you are willing to offer it at. You also want to figure out what price you need to buy it at, so you know how much of a profit you can make when you sell it at the price that they are willing to pay for it. There are many ways to make money by gearing up your business toward eBay sellers. I strongly recommend that as a part of your business, even if you are going to be focusing on the retail aspect of the business, that you investigate ways to make money to eBay sellers.

Chapter 26

Having an auction on eBay is a great way to sell merchandise because you can attract a great number of buyers to your auction. You could have many bidders checking out your auction and if some of them are interested in what you are offering, then some of them will bid on your auction, and you will have a good chance of selling your merchandise for a decent price. You might actually end up making a good amount of money conducting your business. However, selling on eBay is similar to selling in any marketplace. The more people who see your merchandise, the bigger chance that your merchandise will be sold, and also the more money your item(s) could be sold for. In any business situation the equation of supply and demand is true. On eBay, the higher the demand, compared to the supply, the higher the prices will be for the merchandise, or supply.

There are millions and millions of registered users on eBay and an estimated 60,000,000 members. Even though many of those people are looking for the products that you are selling and services you will be offering, unless they are looking at your auction at the time that you are running it, they will not bid. Now while that may seem rather obvious, think about what it really means. Even if there is a store out in California that desperately needs shoelaces because shoelaces sell very well in their market and they can locate them at a desperate price and you might have an entire box of shoelaces being auctioned off at eBay, those shoelaces might have only cost you a penny each and that store in California, which is a registered eBay member, might be willing to spend up to $.10 a shoelace. Even though you have this box of shoelaces that cost you $50.—say you have 5,000 shoelaces—that store in California will be more than happy to pay $500. for the box of shoelaces. Unless they see your auction, they will never bid on it.

So how can you be sure that they will look at your auction? Let me even take it a step further: There can be many more stores that could use those shoelaces and they might all be eBay members, but they just might not be looking at your auction. The reason they might not be looking at your auction is because, maybe that week, they might not be looking at auctions. They might be very busy attending a trade show, or busy dealing with customers, or on holiday, or they just might not have done their diligence on eBay and might not have searched that week because they did not expect to find anything that they needed on eBay that week. So instead, they did not look online and they were concentrating on other venues to obtain the shoelaces they need. If there is a way for you to draw their attention to your eBay auction, then you will have a very good chance of selling the shoelaces for the full price of $.10 a shoelace, maybe even higher, perhaps for $.20 or $.25 apiece, if you get the attention of the interested parties who are eBay members, focusing on your auction.

Up until now, you have only touched upon people who are eBay members. What about all of the people who are not members? I am sure you want to have their business, also. What if there is another shoe store in New Jersey that could use shoelaces, but they have never considered purchasing shoelaces on eBay? They might not even know that there are shoelaces that are offered on eBay. What about a small store in Texas? What about a major buyer for a large retail chain? They might never have even thought to look on eBay because they might have assumed that eBay, as most people assume, is only a business to consumer market plays, where consumer-to-consumer market plays, but not business-to-business market plays. Even though eBay is spending millions and millions of dollars developing their business-to-business section and marketplace, most people in the business-to-business marketplace are not aware of the services and the products that can be found on eBay. If you have seen one of eBay's advertisements, you will notice that they show a vice president for a technological company who obtained a $100,000. worth of brand-new software and hardware that he needed for his company for only 15% of its cost or $15,000. Therefore, if the publics' attentions are drawn to eBay and they see the amazing savings that are offered, even hard-to-please people will be happy to buy merchandise on eBay as long as the price is right. Remember, you do not have to deal with one-on-one negotiating when you sell merchandise through eBay, so it is definitely a great way to sell merchandise, even to the business consumer.

Now, even to retail consumers, people who are just buying the merchandise to use it themselves, so to speak, the end user; the end user also needs merchandise. They might know to look for it on eBay or even if they have an account and is used to looking for that certain type of merchandise. Take for instance a collector of art, who loves checking out eBay every week to see what the latest paintings are being offered for. That collector has become accustomed to finding some great finds from some obscure artists who have beautiful art. Since many of those artists are overlooked, the art can be found for very, very reasonable prices. It is special art that they can show off to their friends and colleagues; and it is definitely art that is not available in the general marketplace. Now, that collector, even though they check eBay every week, they might not check eBay on the specific day that your auction started or ended and might miss your auction altogether. What about someone who loves to build models and is always looking for different model kits to put together? However, just that week, they are away from their computer or not in the mood to search on eBay and misses your great auction for a brand-new model that can be put together in no time at all and is a beautiful boat from the 1800s. Now that person who loves building models would have been more than happy to bid on your boat and might have even wanted to buy it, except since they were not in the mood to look at auctions that week, will simply miss that auction.

Now, every person who misses your auction is one less bidder and one less bidder means less money in your pocket because when his or her bid is not placed, the next bid does not have to be as high as it would have been if that person's bid had been placed. If someone places a bid for $5., the next bid has to be, say, $5.50, but if the bid for $5. has not been placed, then the next bid could still be for $5. The more bidders you attract, the more people will focus on your auction which means the more bids you will receive, the higher the bids will be and the higher the final sale price will be for the item.

So, how do you draw people's attentions to your auctions? Now that you know the importance of having as many eyes looking at your auction as possible, your next step will be to get the public to *focus* on your auction. One way to do that is to build an e-mail contact list of all your previous customers and the people who have sent you inquiries in regards to your auctions. The list should be broken down into sections, depending on the customer inquiry or what customer the customer implied that they needed. If you run auctions for antique books and movies, you will want to have a separate list for the sales and the inquiries that resulted from your auctions for comedies from the 1980s and from antique books from the early 1800s. Once you have that e-mail list, every time you have an auction, you will want to send out an e-mail, letting them know, through a friendly reminder, that you have put up a new item for auction on eBay and why you think this item might interest them. This way, they will see it as a personal contact and they will be glad that you took the time out to contact them to let them know about the auction that you are listing. If the auction simply seems like just an advertisement, then people will be turned-off and might request to be taken off your list, especially if it is not something that they are interested in, then chances are, they will simply ignore your e-mails, from then on.

If they perceive your e-mail as a reminder from someone who enjoys doing business with them and something exciting that they might personally enjoy, even if it is not something they specifically want at that time, they will look forward to your next e-mails. They will know that your e-mails are meant for their advantage. Now, when your customers and the those who sent you inquiries receive an e-mail updating them regarding an auction of something that interests them, they will check out the auction out of curiosity, and want to know what it is that you are offering. If you are offering something that is valuable to them, something that they have enjoyed in the past, then they will go ahead and place a bid. They will also contact you and enter into discussions with you regarding what you have up for sale, even if they decide not to purchase the item in your auction, they might purchase other items that you have in your inventory once you have alerted them to the product that you are offering. As you can see, there are many ways to draw people's attention.

For instance, say someone has a wedding during a certain week and they are too busy to look on eBay because they lack the time or the patience to follow auctions. If you send them an e-mail and point out a specific reason why they should follow the eBay auctions that week, then they will do that. Even if the wedding is three days from that date, and he or she is occupied twenty-four hours a day, let them know that it is a rare item that they can only obtain for the time being, through this one-in-a-lifetime opportunity. It could be a rare antique that you came across at an estate sale somewhere in the south and now you have put it up for sale and people in the north would love to have that old antique that is only available in the southern states, because it is no longer available in 80% of states. As the wedding is coming up, the collector or antique lover will take their time to check out your auction, and may place one bid on the auction. They might, since they are very busy, place a higher bid then they would have, otherwise. The reason that they would place a higher bid is because they know that they will not be able to constantly keep up with the auction and they know that the price of the auction could quickly escalate in value. Therefore, in order not to miss the opportunity to purchase the antique, they will set it at the highest bid that they can afford and then they will walk away and hope that they will win their auction.

Another advantage of contacting people and having them focusing on the auction is the previous example of stores. Say one of those stores want to purchase from you and after weeks and months have gone by, you do not have any contact with those stores because you have not had anything to offer them. So, by putting an e-mail out to them, alerting them to what you are offering, even though months have gone by, if you send out that e-mail and one of the stores happens to need what you are offering them, they are going to be very aggressive in securing the merchandise. Obviously, if you send them an e-mail just at the right time for something that they just happen to need badly, they are not going to be so concerned for what they pay for it, they are going to be more concerned with buying the merchandise so they can resell it and make money.

Say the shoelaces retail for $.30 a pair and you put them up on eBay for your cost and; you know that any bids above your cost is going to mean a profit to you. The store is going to pay more than what you expect them to pay, and they might even pay more than the wholesale price because they need those shoelaces and they cannot get them from their current wholesaler. Yet that store would have never known that you had that auction for the shoelaces unless you sent them an e-mail and alerted them so they could focus on your auction. More than that, they might be so eager to buy those shoelaces from you that they might contact you directly and ask to buy them from you, directly. They might contact you and say, "Hey look, you have this auction for shoelaces. You do not know how high the price will go, and I'm willing to pay as much as $.30 a pair, can we make a deal now?" You end the auction early, send them the shoelaces, and make a good deal of money. If you bought the entire box of 5,000 shoelaces for a penny each, the total cost of the shoelaces was $50. and if you could sell the five thousand shoelaces for $.30 a pair, and in the best scenario, you put about $1,500. in your pocket. There is definitely a lot of room to make money on eBay, and what you need to do is to bring the public's attention to the auctions that you are running.

Another way to conduct business on eBay and, which will lead you to bring the public to your auctions, is to pick up the phone, make a list of all the different types of consumers and business people that would be interested in what you are offering and start contacting them. Make sure that if you are calling up consumers, you check the "do not call" list and follow the laws and regulations that pertain toward telemarketing. The same applies when you call businesses. In the example of where you have shoelaces up for sale on eBay, open up the phone book, call all the shoe stores in you area that carry sneakers and let them know about what you are offering on eBay. If you call 100 stores that carry shoelaces and only four or five of those stores are interested in purchasing them from you, that is still enough customers to give you a good profit. If three or four of those stores start competing against each other to purchase your shoelaces and they drive up the price to $.15 or $.20 a pair, you have still made about 15 times your money. It definitely pays to bring the public's attention to your auctions.

How can you find a list of stores or businesses that focus on the merchandise that you are selling? One way to do that is by going through the phone book, or you could actually accomplish it online, by going to superpages.com, or yellow-pages.com; there are many web sites that allow you to search listings of businesses. After indicating the state that you are looking for, select a city, or you can do it by state only, and put in the key word for the category that the business falls under, *or* you could search by the name of the business.

Say you are selling sneakers and you do not know the name of the business, and you are also not exactly sure what category a certain type of a sneaker store would fall under. You might have exclusive, special sneakers that are only available from a certain country that you imported and now you want to be able to sell them yet you need to find out which store would be your best customer base. So what do you do? You type in the name "sneakers," then you obtain a listing of every store in that state that has the name sneakers as its business name. You might find sneaker wholesalers that way, or sneaker retailers; you also might find distributors of sneakers. Now that you have the entire list, you can pick up the phone, call them and let them know about your auction. When you find a store that is interested in checking out the auction or even a store that just wants to look at pictures of the sneakers, and is considering buying them directly from you, you ask them for their e-mail address, e-mail them either pictures of the sneakers or a link to the auction that you have up for the sneakers. That way, you present the sneakers to them in a professional manner because they will see the photographs and they will be able to follow the auction on eBay.

Many retailers and distributors might not feel comfortable bidding on eBay for merchandise; and they might feel more comfortable buying the merchandise directly without having to compete with many other buyers for obvious reasons. They do not want the price to be driven up; they want to be able to get a good deal without having to worry about missing out on this deal when someone else purchases the merchandise. You could use that to your advantage. You could put 100 sneakers up on eBay for an auction. Maybe you want to sell all of the sneakers in one shot. When someone contacts you and inquiries about buying the merchandise directly from you, you do not have to tell them that you have another 100 sneakers available; or that you have another 1,000 sneakers available. You can set up a deal with them and say, "Look, the sizes of sneakers I have on eBay! I might have some extra sneakers available, how many would you like to take?" You negotiate the price, the quantity and you make your money by making an additional sale. The reason you would do not want to let them know how many pieces you have is because if they know that you have too much of a quantity they might sense that you are in a rush to sell them off, or they might think that you feel pressured to sell your merchandise because you are holding so much of it. Never let people know how many units you have. This way you could also use it to your advantage by telling them this is a product that is extremely hard to find that is not mass-produced. Therefore, if they want it, they need to buy it from you and pay the price you are asking; otherwise you will not be able to buy through another outlet because; there will not be another seller offering the same merchandise you are offering.

Another idea that works very well, is when you are auctioning off an item with a high ticket value or an item you believe can increase in price to a higher level as the bidding increases, is to promote that type of an item through a press release. Sending a press release can be done through either PR News or Business Wire. There is a small charge to send the release online, with a very limited circulation and it will cost around a $100. To send out a press release with a national circulation, it will cost roughly $600. If you were auctioning off a house that you think would appeal to a large number of people due to the fact that a celebrity or a sports figure once lived in that house, you might want to strongly consider sending out a full press release with a national circulation. Even if the press release costs you $600., you might be able to attract so many bidders to your auction that you will make money off the price of the house, including the cost of the press release.

I once saw a house auction on eBay for a house that Kirk Cobain lived in. The price of that house, even though in the same neighborhood the average house sold for roughly $60,000. and the two entrepreneurs who originally bought the house paid $60,000. As the mass media was alerted that this had been the residence of Kirk Cobain while he was growing up, the bidding for this house shot up to over $350,000. because the public was psyched for the opportunity to own the house in which Kirk Cobain grew up. They were so excited that they quickly bid the price beyond its value, based on the neighborhood. They were not concerned with the intrinsic value of the house ; they were more concerned with buying a house where a musician of his caliber—and who they greatly admired—grew up in. If you have something of value that you believe will be appealing to the public on a national scale, based on its attachment to celebrities, or any notoriety it might have, you want to bring as much exposure to that item or service, as possible.

Maybe you are auctioning off the right to have dinner with a famous politician. Say you are auctioning this dinner for a fundraiser for the politicians' chauffeurs or to raise money for charity, and you want to let everybody know that this is a lifetime opportunity to have dinner with a particular famous politician. You are offering two hours of the politician's time, and while their time is valuable, if you were just selling it to a very limited audience, people might be willing to pay for those two hours of time. Even if they are willing to pay for the time, they might only want to pay $100. or $200. for the right to sit down and enjoy a two hour dinner. In reaching out to a national audience, however, there might be so many people who admire that politician, and are curious to meet them with their list of questions for the politician. These people might want to share their ideas with this particular politician and the bidding for that auction could be in the thousands of dollars.

I once saw bidding for the right to have dinner with Warren Buffet go over $11,000. for just one person. The total price for the auction was over $80,000. for the right for eight people to sit down and have dinner with Warren Buffet. You see, there is a lot of potential in eBay, especially when you can market your auction properly and alert the people who are interested in what you may have. Remember, you want to focus on both active and non-active eBay members. Focusing on people who have no connection to eBay can be productive as well, because once you alert them to what it is that you are offering, they could become excited and they will have a strong incentive to check out your auction. When they otherwise would not have bid on your auction, they might decide to bid on it.

An innovative method to put into action is to advertise your auction through regular media outlets, such as on the radio, in the newspaper, or on cable TV. It is possible to could get spots that are not during prime-time where you can obtain the time for a very cheap price. Make sure you are advertising the auction at least one or two weeks before the auction runs and if people are excited enough about what you are offering, they will mark it on their calendar and they will check it out. When you advertise in the mass media, through an e-mail newsletter, the radio, TV, a banner campaign, a mail order campaign, or through direct mail, when you actually mail out letters, it is important to receive responses back. You want people to call you, and to have them give you their e-mail addresses and phone numbers. That way you can contact them when it is time for the auction or to remind them of your upcoming great auction that you are having, and the public will be informed and hopefully bid on your auction. As long as you are reaching as many people as possible who are interested in what it is that you are offering, there are many methods through which you can contact people. As long as the medium through which you advertise to reach people still reaches the niche that you want to reach, you are in good shape. It would not be smart to advertise an auction for a fishing rod to a vegetarian web site. On the same hand, advertising a television on an e-mail list that is geared towards book lovers, would not get you very far. The item that you are offering and the advertising medium that you are using should, in the best scenario, complement each other and help you reach the market that will be receptive to the merchandise or services you are offering on eBay.

I remember seeing a press release by a company that was conducting a million dollar auction on eBay. Even though the auction had already finished, they made the decision to put out a press release so that the public would know that if they were interested in collectible coins,. that specific company was a good place to purchase them. That way, people make sure to check on future auctions to see what other coins this company is selling. Another reason they sent out the press release was in the possible case of someone who plans to sell their coins contacting this company and perhaps setting up a consignment sale allowing them to sell their coins on eBay. Obviously, if this company sold a million dollars worth of coins on eBay, they know what they are doing. When they do sell coins on eBay, they make money as the seller, who sent out the press release, and the people or person who originally contacted them and gives them their coins to sell, will also make money in selling those coins. Keeping people apprised of your auctions before and after they happen is a wise idea. The reason you want to keep them apprised before they happen, of course, is so that they focus and bid on your auction. The reason you want to apprise the public *after* the auction has been completed, is if they have merchandise that they want to get rid of that is similar to the merchandise you have sold, they can sell it to you. When people read about your auction, they can look forward to participating in it and in the future, will stay in touch with you and your business to keep track of what auctions you have that pertain to the areas in which they are interested.

Chapter 27

At this point in the book, you have received more than enough information to start an eBay business and to have a very good chance at becoming quite successful at it. If you plug in the information that you have learned from this book, you can find yourself developing a full-time income, in no time at all. In just a short period of time, you could replace your full-time or part-time income. There are many people who support themselves full-or part-time from the income that they receive on eBay. There are even individuals that make six-figure incomes on eBay and businesses that reach in the millions of dollars with the revenue exclusively derived from their eBay businesses. You can be one of those people, if you work at it! Unfortunately, it is not enough to know how to run an eBay business, you also need to learn what to sell. While you might have all of your sales skills in order, to develop your eBay business and start making money with it, you need something to sell, whether it is a service or a product. I am sure you will agree that without having the actual assets to deliver, whether it is a service or a product, you are not going to be able to generate any income.

In order for you to become successful and have something to sell, it's vital to know what sells well on eBay. Therefore, this chapter will be devoted to the hottest selling products on eBay. The hottest products on eBay are the same products that sell *off* eBay. You have to ask why people go to eBay. If you want to figure out what sells really well, find out who the average customer is. Find out not only who the customer is and what it is that he or she is looking for, also why that customer would feel compelled to shop on eBay, as opposed to other online web sites, or, for that matter, any off-line retailers. There are reasons why the public shops on eBay, spends time following auctions and looking through the different auctions, spends time bidding on the auctions, responding to sellers, and then determining if the item that is being offered is for them, or not. As you can see, whatever it is you are offering on eBay has to be appealing enough that someone would shop on eBay, and purchase your item with risks that they personally take.

As opposed to simply buying that item or a similar product on another online web site, or through an off-line channel, such as a retail outlet, a shopping mall, a large retailer, or a large department store. There are many reasons why the public would buy from you on eBay and it is up to you to come up with a good reason for them to select your product.

Here are some ideas. The reason the public might shop on eBay, to some extent, is that the item they want is not being offered through the buyer's local retail channels, other online web sites, or the product is special enough that although the product is being offered somewhere else, the person is so anxious to buy it, they are happy to pay the price you are offering it for. Therefore, they would rather purchase that option on eBay instead of purchasing the option through another online web site or retail channel. If the product is being offered at a good price on eBay, the public will want to buy it on eBay, as opposed to another online web site. If the item is an exclusive product or being offered at a very, very cheap price as compared to a retail outlet, then that consumer would most probably purchase the product on eBay.

Say the consumer is located in a rural town in Arkansas and does not have access to a large shopping mall, such as the type you might have access to, if you lived in Philadelphia. Now, that consumer living in the rural town in Arkansas, would be willing to purchase products that would be found in that local shopping mall where you live. The reason they would be willing to purchase those items and even at a similar price that they would pay at a department store; it is because they do not have much of a choice. They might not want to drive thirty minutes to find that product at a local mall, when they could just order the product through eBay, wait for it to arrive and have the product delivered straight to their home. Say they are not in a rush to buy themselves a brand-new stereo and they do not mind if they have a stereo one week or the next and the only other alternative for them is to drive to Wal-Mart. To get to Wal-Mart, it is at least forty-five minutes by car. So, that buyer would much rather place his order on eBay, hopefully win the item, and wait for it to arrive; they do not have to take any time out of their busy schedule to obtain the product; the product arrives directly to their home or business. So, what would make that a hot item for that person? In order to make it hot, it needs to be easily accessible; a convenient item to order, arrive directly to their residence or business, would be offered at a much better price then it would at any local store, and would be offered cheaper than on another online web site. So you can see, in order for a product to be hot for a buyer, it does not have to be a hot product per say, but hot, personally, to that buyer.

What other items sell very well on eBay? By a similar token, a VCR or a stereo could sell well for consumers who are based in rural areas. Collectibles sell really well for the same reason, on eBay. You see a collectible is a product that cannot be easily bought or located through retail channels or online web sites. Say you are selling a box of vintage basketball cards, on eBay. Someone who may be considering buying the cards does not have many options, because finding those particular vintage basketball cards online, is not easy. They also cannot walk into their local basketball card shop, if there is such a thing, and purchase the cards. Therefore, if you offer the cards at a good decent price, there is more of a chance that person will offer to buy the cards. They will be willing to spend their money on the cards, and go ahead and purchase them. Whatever it is that you are selling, on eBay, it needs to be appealing. What makes an item appealing? When the item is hard to obtain or when you cannot simply go to a local store and find it. For that reason, collectibles sell like hot cakes, on eBay. Simply because the collectible that is being offered is exclusive to the degree that it cannot be found anywhere else and even if it *could* be found in other locations, the further a person is away from a metropolitan center, the less of a chance there is that person will be able to find that collectible.

You see, while the baseball card, comic book, record, and antique shows are in most city and metropolitan areas, the farther away the public is from those metropolitan areas, the harder it is to find those types of shows. Even if they have an antique show in a rural area, they might not have the same selection as an antique show in a metropolitan area. If you could offer good merchandise that would normally be found in an antique show or at a baseball card show on eBay, then you will have many potential bidders who will be interested in purchasing the products. The key is to make sure that what you are offering is something which is appealing to bidders, because the public might not have easy access to it, and you are offering it cheaper than your competitors while the price is good and the item is a rare one.

There are other ways to determine what is hot on eBay. Go on eBay and see which products are selling the most, notice what the most listings are for a given product; this is something you can search for yourself. Look at different product categories and notice the items within the categories and which are receiving the highest bids. If there is an item receives a high bid consistently, then you know it is a hot selling product and one that you need to focus on. Now, say you are in a situation where you are not having any luck in finding hot products on eBay. Say you are looking at eBay and you suddenly feel overwhelmed, because it seems that in every category, there are products that sell well products that do not sell well. That would give you the correct answer or idea to what is a hot selling product. The other thing you can do in order to determine if the product you want to sell is a hot seller, is to visit trade shows and see which products are selling very well. Usually whatever sells well online will also sell well off-line. You want to find out what products are selling well at trade shows, different stores and after doing your research online, find out what the hottest products are. If you know anyone in retail, ask them, say, what is your best seller, this season?

Once you locate what the item is, find a source for the merchandise and start selling it on eBay. Do not stock up too much on the product because once you do, and the fad changes and that product is no longer hot, you will be left holding a large inventory of an item that no longer sells. How can you be certain that the product sells well? The best way is to check on eBay and see for yourself what is selling well, and remember one thing: people are the same, everywhere. If something is selling well off-line, it will also sell well online, and you can provide the product under the same circumstances, off-line. Say there is a product off-line that is doing well because people can gain access to it very quickly and can receive a high quality item—then you want to be in the same situation when you sell the merchandise online. Make sure that the people receiving the merchandise online will also be able to receive the same merchandise in a very efficient and quick manner. As you can see, in order to know what you need to sell on eBay, first investigate what is selling best on and off eBay—once you know what that product is, you will be on your way to developing a system where you have hot selling products.

A good way to have a constant stream of hot selling products is to put your name out there and to stay in touch with wholesalers, brokers, sales representatives from companies, and to always ask them to give you a list of what the hottest selling products are, then tell them you are interested in buying those products. If you want to be able to buy those products, your name needs to be familiar. You need to have sales agents, sales representatives, manufacturers' reps, wholesalers, retailers, discounters, liquidators, know that you are always active in the market, ready to buy merchandise and if they have any for you, you will buy it without hesitation. If you can develop a reputation for someone who buys in large volumes and is always eager to buy, you will have many offers coming your way. Similar to Wal-Mart, they receive thousands of offers for products, everyday. If you develop a good reputation as a solid buyer who is looking for merchandise, you will have offers from many different sellers whether they are liquidators, wholesalers, or manufacturers, for hot selling merchandise. Always be on the lookout for the next fad.

To determine what merchandise is considered a fad, turn on MTV. Watch it, see what it is that people are buying. Go to your local supermarket, see which isles are always running out of merchandise, and what kind of merchandise is offered in those isles. Remember opening up a local newspaper will show you the kinds of merchandise that is selling well in your area. Realize that if it is selling well in your area, there must be other areas around the world that would be interested in having the same merchandise. If lawnmowers do well in your area during the summer, it would be a safe bet that they do well in similar areas during the summer. If people ski in your area, all you need to do is stock up on ski supplies and find other areas where people also ski. Then you put offer that merchandise on eBay, all of the various skiing supplies and then hopefully buyers will buy the merchandise from you, provided that you are offering good quality merchandise that is priced reasonably. If you want to develop a good, solid eBay business and build that business, you need to make sure that you are always in touch with pop culture. You need to see what is it that people on the street enjoy buying, and then you need to gear yourself up so you can obtain that merchandise and get ready to sell those items. If doing this, you will have an easy time finding a good stream of hot selling products and you especially want to be able to find those products before your competition finds them. Once your competition finds the same merchandise, you will be competing based on price and while you can always differentiate yourself based on service, once your competition is offering the same merchandise, you will not have that extra edge of having hot selling merchandise that your competition does not have. So in order to make yourself a leader in the field, you want to be able to jump on the hot fad while it is in fashion. Act quickly, find that hot selling merchandise before your competition does, and then start selling it as quickly as possible—this way you can be the first player in the market with the hot merchandise that you are introducing or selling on eBay.

Chapter 28

When you run your eBay business, you are going to encounter aspects of the business world that you find in both in the online and the off-line world. One important aspect to know how to deal with is learning what to do when a dispute arises. While most of the time there should not be any disputes, but you might want to be prepared when a dispute arises. Among the types of disputes that are common on eBay, is when a buyer is unhappy with a description of an item, or a seller is unhappy with the amount of payment that they actually receive or their is a delay in payment. The seller can also be unhappy with the correspondence from the buyer or the buyer could also be unhappy with the correspondence from the seller, maybe the buyer has waited too long to receive his merchandise and they expected to receive the merchandise before they actually did. You see, there are potentially things that could take place in a transaction that could enrage the buyer and the seller.

As one who sells, your job is to diffuse the tension when a dispute starts. Try to resolve things as soon as possible. The reason you want to resolve the situation is not even so much as to satisfy the buyer, even though you should have as a priority the desire to satisfy the buyer—what you also want to make sure is that you do not receive any negative feedback. If the person you are doing business with puts negative feedback on your account and other people who want to do business with first check out your account, they will see that that you have negative feedback. They are going to be very cautious about doing business with you and many people who would have otherwise bid on your auction, will not bid on your auction when they see that you have negative feedback. Therefore, your job as an eBay seller is to do whatever you need to do to ensure that you do not receive any negative feedback.

In situations when someone is upset with your auction, you still want to try to resolve things as diplomatically as possible to ensure that you are left with positive feedback. Even if you are 100% in the right and it is very frustrating to deal with that particular buyer who, and I might agree with you in many situations, is too demanding or their demands are not realistic. This will help you with future sales. For instance, when you are trying to send something out as soon as possible and you have indicated beforehand, that it will take two or three days for the item to be sent out. UPS or the postal office will take an additional four or five days to deliver the merchandise to the buyer, and in a situation like that where the buyer is still unhappy that they did not receive the merchandise as soon as they wanted it delivered to him explain the situation patiently, apologize for the delay and let the buyer know why it took so long. You see, instead of accusing the buyer of being unreasonable and straight out that it was not in your control, let them know that you did your part and that is just the way life is; it takes four to five days for the merchandise to be delivered. While giving over that information and arguing from that point of view, you would be correct, you would have done your part and there really is nothing legally or ethically the buyer could hold over you. Since you are in business to make money and you are in business for the long term, you might even decide to solicit more business from this buyer and from future buyers that this person could refer you to. So think of it as your obligation, your responsibility—and go ahead and do what you need to do to resolve this situation in the best way possible. In order to be able to take care of the situation, you need to take that extra step.

One of the things you could always do is tell the buyer, "Hey look, even though I did my best with the shipping, I still realize that you are unhappy with the time period that it took to have your merchandise to be delivered. What I am willing to do the next time you place an order, is to give you an extra bonus that will compensate for the delay in sending this order." If the buyer is reasonable and 99% of the buyers are reasonable, the buyer will be happy that you are taking the time and putting in the effort to make sure that they are happy with the transaction, especially when you offer to send them a free bonus in the next transaction. In that situation, the buyer should have no complaints and should be more than happy to give you positive feedback since they know that you are trying to make him happy. By offering to send them an extra bonus with their next order, you are giving an extra incentive to be satisfied and to give you positive feedback.

Say that the buyer is so upset that for some reason they do not want to place another order with you until this situation is 100% resolved. In that situation, you could start out by offering to send the buyer a free bonus right away, as long as the buyer is willing to pay the cost of the shipping. So what you do is select a bonus that is an item that really did not cost you much or you might have even picked up for free, offer to send that item out to the buyer and have them, as a fair compromise, pay for the cost of the shipping. If the buyer is still reluctant to pay for the cost of the shipping and you feel that you have gone out of your way to satisfy this buyer just so they will give you positive feedback, send them the free bonus and pay for the shipping yourself, out of your own pocket. Do it because this person might not reorder from you, because at this point, it does not seem like this is a serious buyer and chances are, might not plan to reorder from you no matter what you do, but you do this to salvage your reputation. As long as the buyer is satisfied with your treatment of them, most likely they will give you positive feedback, which will help you in your future business endeavors on eBay.

While you are trying to set up your business in a way where all buyers that you interact with will be happy, it is not always likely to happen. You will have buyers who for one reason or another will be unhappy. Say there is a buyer on eBay who feels that the merchandise you sent was misrepresented. Take the approach you did before, and offer to send the buyer additional merchandise that he or she will be happy with as long as they pay for the cost of shipping. Remind them that, in fact, you did not misrepresent the merchandise, you are not legally bound to send them more merchandise, and you are willing to because you want to make them happy. You do it because you want to have their future business. The only thing that you ask of them is that they cover the cost of the shipping for the merchandise. If they are not willing to do that, depending on how much you want their business in the future and how much it means to you to have positive feedback, you could keep negotiating down. Keep extending more benefits and options, offer to pay for the cost of shipping, or they can split the cost half way with you. You can always add more benefits and features until you resolve the situation. While you want to resolve the situation as soon as possible, you also do not want to lose money on the deal you made with them. There are no advantages to going out of your way to satisfy this buyer if you are giving up all of the profits that you made with this transaction. Realize that people understand that on eBay, from time to time, you receive negative feedback. As long as you respond to the negative feedback on your profile with a good reason why you did not deserve that negative feedback, most people will understand. If you are still concerned with any of your auction descriptions, you could let people know why you received that negative feedback. Say for instance, you received the negative feedback because the merchandise you sent out was not properly packed.

In that situation, you need to list in all of your auction descriptions that you are now using a new innovative packing method that helps the merchandise arrive in top condition. This way, even if someone reads a negative feedback and sees that in the past you sent out the merchandise without having it packed properly, they will see that you have resolved this issue and the merchandise that you are now sending out is packed properly. That way, the public will not have an issue with you and people will happy to deal with you. The key is to make sure you are able to supply people with a mechanism to resolve the disputes. By resolving the disputes that arise or offering people a way to resolve the disputes, will encourage people to be more understanding, when issues arise. If the public feels that they can contact you and there is an open communication process, then even if they are not happy with the merchandise that they receive, the first thing they will do is contact you to resolve the situation. What they will not do is rush to give you negative feedback or to complain to eBay about your business dealings because they know that you are an individual that is honest and sincere and you are willing to resolve their situation. Remember to keep a balance in wanting to resolve the situation, making sure that you make money with your auction. While you do want to make money with the auction, you also need to make sure that in the future you receive more business from this individual and other eBay buyers.

I once conducted business with an individual who was not that thrilled with the variety of merchandise he received. Since this individual placed a very large order, I offered three boxes of merchandise free, in his next order. That way he was ensured that the next time he ordered, he would receive a better variety of merchandise. I said to him, "If this is an issue for you this time, I can make sure to resolve it by the next time we do business together, by giving you a better variety of merchandise. What I can also do is to go ahead and give you three boxes for free, immediately, to make up for the lack of merchandise that you feel you received during the last time that you did business with me." In this way, I was able to resolve the situation and this person felt I was being honest by addressing the issue. He was a satisfied customer and instead of just walking away as an angry buyer, he turned around and purchased merchandise from me, again. Both of us came out ahead because in the next transaction, this individual paid less for the shipping because I offered to pay for some of the shipping out of my own pocket, he also received three boxes of free merchandise including a good variety, making him a satisfied customer. It was worthwhile for me, even though in the next transaction, I made a very small amount of money, because I kept him as a long-term customer and I was able to receive positive feedback. That was helpful to me in future sales and I was able, from experience, to know that I needed to satisfy possible future buyers who end up happy with what I sell to them.

If you do receive negative feedback, and it is too late, you want the public to know that you are resolving the situation, and you want to respond to the negative feedback in your profile. What I would not recommend—which I made a mistake doing, one time—is rushing to put negative feedback on his or her profile. If you put negative feedback on their profile, all it will seem like is that you both to an extent have a legitimate reason to be upset with each other—but people like to stay away from arguments. Therefore, if you are involved in an argument with someone else, people might think, "You know what? I am really not sure who is right and who is wrong, but I really do not want anything to do with either the buyer or the seller because it is questionable the way they are conducting their businesses." However, you can stay above the fray and do not respond with negative feedback, and show people that you really did try to resolve the situation. Then even the negative feedback will be to your credit because people might say, "Look at what a good individual this person is, they received negative feedback, and since they really wanted to resolve this in a businesslike and diplomatic fashion, they did not go ahead and give the other party in the transaction negative feedback." By abstaining from giving negative feedback, even when it is well deserved, you are putting yourself on a higher rung that will discourage other eBay buyers to want to do business with you. So make sure you come out ahead and you look clean and that whatever it is you are doing is honest and if there is a situation that arises, try to find the proper way to resolve the situation.

In many situations, even when you know you are 100% right, realize that the value of having a good reputation and work with the other party to ensure that they are happy. Maintain your intact relationship and even if it costs you some extra money now, keep in mind that if you develop your eBay business properly, it could turn into a six-figure income, if not higher. I know when you are just starting out a business that every dollar counts and you might be very reluctant to give up any of your profits to satisfy a buyer especially when you know that you are right and the buyer is in the wrong. So make sure that you have your eyes out on the big picture and that you do not mind giving up some of the profits now in the desire and hope of having a lot more business in the future. Remember if you want to build a six-figure income on eBay, in order to do that, you are going to have to have a very clean slate. If you have more then one or two negative feedback, you are going to have a very hard time building your business to the extent to start making serious money for yourself. You do not want to be held back by those negative feedback. Therefore, the lesson you should learn from this chapter and keep your focus on the future. Think about you need out of the future and to resolve any situation as quickly as possible, so you can move forward and set your aims high and take that step closer to becoming a successful eBay business person.

Chapter 29

Once an auction has been completed on eBay, the top bidder will want to know how to pay you. Deciding on what methods of payment you will be accepting that major factor that will influence your success on eBay. You see, aside from the actual auction and your reputation on eBay, your success will also depend on how much revenue you receive and what percentage of that revenue you will keep. For example, depending on how someone pays you, you will be receiving either 100% of that payment or you will be receiving that payment minus a small percentage. That percentage could be a user fee, a commission, or it could be a credit card user fee.

Say someone pays you with a credit card and your credit card keeps a 2% processing fee per transaction; then you will only be receiving 98% of the revenue. Based on that, you might decide that you only will accept money orders, personal checks, bank checks, cashiers checks, or business checks because this way, you can keep 100% of the revenue. Now, the downside of that is some people might not feel so comfortable sending you payment where they might not have any recourse if the auction is not good. Say for example, someone buys a guitar from you, and they send you a check. You wait the six to seven days for the check to clear, the check clears, you send them the guitar. They are going to be worried the whole time that if they do not like the guitar for some season or you do not even send the guitar to them, that they might not receive the merchandise and they will not have any way to collect the money they sent you. People are very concerned with losing money they spend on auctions. You will want to be careful and to make sure that people feel comfortable doing business with you and that they trust you. To prove you are trustworthy, show them that you are also taking a chance and by taking a chance, you are giving them an option to reclaim the funds that they are sending you if the need arises.

If someone pays with a credit card, they know that if the situation of fraud arises, they can contact the credit card company and void their payment to you. The charge will not be on their statement and the money is taken out of your bank account or your credit card account, as you may have your account set up. Now, the thing about accepting a credit card from an eBay buyer is that once you send that guitar out and it is a great guitar in super working condition, if the buyer is not interested in paying for that guitar, they can dispute the charge and if they successfully dispute the charge, then you are out of your guitar and money that you received for that guitar. If, for any fraudulent reason, their credit card is not good, or valid, or the credit card is being used by someone who is not authorized to use, the owner of that credit card can dispute the charge, and you will also be out of your money and not have the guitar, either. You want to find a way where you could accept payment, and you are also protecting yourself.

So, how can you do that? Is there a way to do that besides accepting a money order or a check? Yes, there actually is. The way you could offer security to both yourself and the buyer is by using PayPal. PayPal is an online electronic banking system that allows people to send and receive money by e-mail. You set up an account, deposit money into your account and then send money directly from your account to other people or you could also send people money by adding a credit card to the account. When you send money from your account to someone else's account, the money will be taken out of your credit card, charged to your credit card and then the recipient will receive the money. You could also send an electronic check. An electronic check is when you have money in your bank account, your bank account will be linked to PayPal and PayPal sends money to a recipient. PayPal will withdraw money from your bank account and over the course of three to four days, will send the money to the person who you would like to receive that money.

The way that PayPal prevents fraud is by validating the user. If someone is a confirmed user and has given a confirmed address, PayPal knows that the credit card that they are using belongs to that person and they have gone ahead and done what they need to do to validate that the person who is using this account is at a certain address. Now, how do they ensure that when you actually send the merchandise out, it is going to the person who owns the credit card? Because you can only send the merchandise to the confirmed address, the address that matches the ownership of the credit card and of the PayPal account. You can send the merchandise to whatever address you want, and you will no longer be protected by PayPal if you send it to an unconfirmed address. The type of protection that PayPal gives you is if the person who purchases the merchandise using the credit card has the merchandise delivered to their confirmed address; if that individual disputes the purchase and says they never made the purchase, and that someone else used their credit card fraudulently, PayPal will not take the money out of your account, they will let you keep the funds that you received from the buyer and they take the loss themselves or they attempt to pursue it, until they resolve it.

The downside about using PayPal is that PayPal charges a percentage as a transaction fee from any money you receive in your account. If a seller receives money through PayPal, when the money actually shows up in the seller's PayPal account, it will be minus a small transaction fee. The transaction fee can range anywhere from 1% to 2.55% and in addition there could be a $1. or $.50 charge per transaction. This transaction fee can change from time to time, it can change depending on what competition PayPal has or does not have, in the future. PayPal, like any other business, wants to stay competitive and the transaction fees that they charge will be dependent on the marketplace. The 2.55% transaction fee might not seem like a large price to pay to receive money through PayPal and in many instances it is worth it, even if you have to give 2.5 % of every transaction. The reason that its worth it is because many buyers who, otherwise, would not bid on your auction, would not feel comfortable sending you money, and will now be willing to purchase merchandise from you, because they know they have the safety of using PayPal.

How are they protected by using PayPal? If they send you money and you never send out the merchandise at all, they can always contact PayPal and have the funds returned to their account. You want to be able to make sure that the bidders who see your auctions feel comfortable and acknowledge that you are a trustworthy individual, that you have set up your account and your transaction in a way that allows them and yourself to be protected. While you want to offer this protection to encourage bidders to join your auction and to purchase items from you, you also want to minimize the fee. Especially when you compare the 2.55% fee, with not having to pay any fee at all for the money you receive, such as if you receive the money with a check or money order, then in that situation you would not be giving up any of that percentage. When you take 2.55% and multiply that by 50 auctions that you will be doing on eBay, you will realize that 50 times 2.55% is already over 100%. So, for every 50 or forty-five auctions you will be running on eBay, you will be actually giving away one free auction because every time you receive $100., you will be loosing $2.55; multiply that by forty auctions, and you are out $100. Which, really you did receive, but because PayPal kept on deducting $2.55 from every transaction, you are eventually out $100. In addition to that, eBay takes about a 3% fee from the end of every transaction.

Say you sell an item for $100., eBay will charge you a $3. fee at the end of an auction, based on the percentage of what you sold. When you combine the 3% that eBay charges with the 2.55% that PayPal charges, you are out 5.5% of every transaction that you conduct on eBay. Now, it is not the end of the world because if you are working on at least a 50% profit margin or a 100% markup, 5% of every transaction is not a very high price to pay when you look at the fact that you are receiving a lot of benefits from using eBay and PayPal. If you do not use eBay you save the 3%, but then you do not get any of the business that you would be receiving by doing business on eBay. You could say to yourself, "Hey look, if I do not use PayPal, I do not have to give up 2.55%, but then on the other hand, I will not receive any of the additional business that would have been received by the sellers and the buyers who use PayPal when they conduct business with me." It is to your advantage to use both PayPal and eBay.

Here's a strategy that I have developed in order to offer buyers the security and confidence of using PayPal, and at the same time, I receive my funds, 90% of the time, without having to give up any of the revenues to PayPal. How do I do this? On every auction, I allow people to pay with PayPal. I tell them very clearly, and I state on the auction that if they are a PayPal member, if they have a confirmed address and are a verified user, I am more then happy to except their payments through PayPal. On the other hand, I let them know that I would prefer that they pay with a money order or personal check. In order to encourage them to pay me with a personal check or money order as opposed to PayPal, I either offer them a slight discount, if they pay with a money order or personal check or I give them an extra bonus.

Now you might ask, "If you are giving them a slight discount when they are paying with a money order, then isn't that the same as if they had just paid you with PayPal and you lost the 2.5%?" You see the difference is, when I offer them the discount, I do not offer a 2.5% discount, I offer them a 2% discount because it allows me to still save a .5% on every transaction, that I otherwise would have had to pay to PayPal. PayPal, which is owned by eBay, will charge me 2.55% of any funds that I receive through them. If I receive my funds through a check or a money order and I only give up 2% of my funds, then I am still .5% ahead. That .5% adds up because it means that for every $100., I save $.50. Now, $.50 does not seem like a lot, but if you are conducting $10,000. worth of transactions on a monthly basis, then that .5% comes out to an extra $50. Especially if you look at $50. throughout the course of the year, that is an extra $600. in your pocket.

Moreover, if you are conducting a business as some of the large eBay businesses are, where they are running millions of dollars worth of auctions a year, then that .5% becomes thousands and thousands of dollars. This strategy *can work*!

When you accept a money order or a personal check, you do not even have to offer people a 2% discount. Or even a 1% discount because once you show them that you are honest and explain to them why you would rather receive the money through a money order or a check, they will realize that you are not trying to defraud them. Why? Because you are offering them the PayPal option and if you make it very clear to them that if the reason you would rather receive your funds with a money order or a check is so that you can avoid the percentage that PayPal deducts, most people will understand that. Most people understand that since they are sending you the full $100., that you want to receive the full $100. and because PayPal deducts the percentage fee from all of the funds that you receive, they will also eat the money that covers the cost of shipping. You see, if someone sends you $100. for the merchandise and another $100. for the cost of shipping, PayPal does not care why someone is sending you money, they will deduct the 2.55% from both $100s. You are actually out of $2.55 for the shipping costs and you will have to put money out of your own pocket to cover the $2.55 for the shipping. Once again, $2.55 does not sound like a lot, but if you are conducting a hundred transactions or more a month, then you are talking about $255. a month, then through out the course of the year, $3,000. Therefore, you do want to try to eliminate all of your costs and to manage your expenses when you have an opportunity to do so.

Another option is you could give people free bonuses if they agree to send you a money order or a check. You want to make sure that those free bonuses, including the shipping cost, does not add up to the 2.55% or the 2% discount that you would have given them otherwise, then it would not be worthwhile to give them those extra bonuses. You can say to yourself that you planned to give them a free bonus anyway and you had already figured the cost of sending them a free bonus into the sale price of the auction. If you did that and you were already going to send them a fee bonus, then you might as well let them know that the free bonus is being sent to them in appreciation of them not paying you through PayPal, as well. That way people will understand that you are doing something for them, you are going out of your way for them and most people will reciprocate, and meet your needs by going ahead and paying through the method that you are requesting.

One method of receiving your money, although there is fee that is deducted for it, is receiving a wire transfer. A wire transfer is safe to the extent that it is documented who is receiving it and who is sending it out, but once the money has been sent out, it is very hard to ever retrieve the money and it might not actually be possible. Be careful and I would not recommend listing on your auction that you accept wire transfers because most people do not understand what a wire transfer is. They associate it with an offshore bank account or some other unscrupulous business dealing and they will be very hesitant to do business with you if they see that option. At the same time, you might offer the PayPal option and a check option, and I still recommend staying away from including a wire transfer on your auction.

These are the best methods, although there are other methods such as Billpoint. The eBay site owns their own credit card processing method, and there are many other third party providers—a company called XOOM, which will allow you to send a money order through their online system. Therefore, always keep in mind what the benefits are of offering each option and the cost. When you offer an option, think of what it will do as far as increasing the amount of bids and business you will receive and compare it to the cost that you will be giving up through commissions and transaction fees that you will have to give to those processing providers.

Chapter 30

So now you have received a solid education on how to run an eBay business. I would not be surprised if the biggest question on your mind now is, "But can I take this information, implement it, utilize it, and set myself up a business that can give me a full time income?" I would strongly suggest that the answer is a solid "yes" with one condition and that condition is that if you decide to dedicate yourself and put the effort in, then you are going to need to set up an eBay business. You see, setting up an eBay business requires the same amount of effort as setting up any type of business. It might not require the same type of financial investment as opening up a McDonald's or a gas station, but it does require the same mental effort and the same perseverance and persistence that you would need in any type of business. It is going to take many hours of trying out different strategies, different tips that will be suggested in this chapter, and you are going to have to try out different methods that have already been covered, until you find the exact system that works for you.

Moreover, once you have that system, you are going to have to continuously refine your plan as the marketplace changes. Even as different products become popular and other products lose out, you are going to have to monitor your business to make sure that you have the right merchandise that fits in with what people want today. You are going to have to make sure that you move out the merchandise that is starting to become slow-moving merchandise since you do not want to have anything that you cannot sell. While conducting your business, you are also going to become familiar with the term "service providers," that are going to enable you to succeed with your business. You will find auction management software, software that eBay and other technological providers provide, that allows you to put up many different auctions at once. It can allow you to put up from 100 to 500 auctions at once, with the press of a key. Say you are putting up 30 auctions for 30 different products. This way every time you put those auctions back up, instead of having to retype all the auctions and the headlines for those auctions, with the click of the button you can instantly submit all 30 auctions and have them up at once.

As your business progresses, you will also discover different payment methods. As was covered, you can use PayPal, XOOM, Billpoint, or you might decide to use an escrow account. You see, there are many different items and technologies available and different strategies that you will learn as you become immersed in your business. Once you start utilizing the research that you have, you will be able to gain more of the marketplace and produce more revenue. When I mention revenue, the next question on your mind might be, "Is it really possible for me to make money on eBay?" After all, the reason you are starting an eBay business is to make money with it.

To answer that, let us go over some examples of people who are actually making real money on eBay. I recently read an article in *Entrepreneur Magazine* of an individual who sells pool tables to people. He used to have billiards and he is selling a few pool tables a month, to different people who want to have pool tables at home. He tried, just by chance, figuring he would auction off a pool table on eBay. Over the course of a month, he auctioned off two or three pool tables and said to himself, "There seems to be a business over here!" Within three months, he closed his shop, exclusively devoted his business toward selling pool tables, and eBay became his only outlet. He expects to gross $15,000.000. this year. I know of a computer liquidator that sells $250,000. worth of computers every year on eBay. There is also a woman who sells fancy clothing, that you would normally find in an upscale shop or small boutique located in an exclusive area—she makes over $500,000. worth of sales a year with a profit margin of over 50%. There are individuals who support themselves full-time selling packing supplies on eBay for other eBay sellers. I know of an individual who has a business exclusively selling refurbished electronic, on eBay. This individual sells $5,000 to $10,000 worth of refurbished electronics in any given month. Therefore, there are people who are not only supporting themselves with eBay sales, they are earning over six or seven figures!

As long as you can devote yourself to your business and practice persistence, you can learn everything there is to know about your business. Not only will you be making money with what you currently do on eBay, you will be exposed to new opportunities. Being flexible with you business is a necessity so as a new area becomes popular or as you find new merchandise, you could quickly adapt and include that merchandise or that service into your present eBay business expanding your revenue level and making you more money. What I would advise is not to let your business grow too quickly because many businesses whether they are online or off-line, face tough times due to having too much growth too soon. By too much growth, they take too much on themselves; and either purchase too much inventory, which they might have a hard time selling, they will also take on too many financial obligations, which they cannot cover.

Say, for instance, a store is starting to do well and the owner says, "Look—you know, since we're currently making $50,000. a year with one shop, let's open up a second store and it'll double our revenue." Then they are not very careful with the second store. They do not pick as good of a location like they did with the first store and instead of making money with the second store, they lose money, and then the profits from the first store are needed to cover the lease and the other business expenses for the second store. The same thing can happen with your eBay business. Say your business is slowly growing and you say to yourself, "You know what? I could easily afford to hire a third or fourth employee to help out with my business." Now you hire those employees, and pay them a salary, and then it turns out that your business is not doing well enough to support their salaries. Therefore, their salaries will be coming out of the profits from the rest of your business and it might even have to come out of your pocket if the business starts slowing down.

Some people rent a small warehouse for their eBay business before they really need that space. What I would suggest is if you could start out by working from your basement, garage, or even your spare bedroom, you do that until you have no choice but to expand and even when you do need additional storage space, first check in your neighborhood if someone has a garage for rent. I have seen many garages rent for as little as $150. a month. That is a lot cheaper then anything you will find at any storage facility. Your next option could be a storage facility, where you could rent a 10 x 10 foot space or 20 x 20, for $300. to $400. a month and depending on your area, it might be a little less or a little more. If your business is really taking off, where you need to have plenty of space to store the merchandise, pack, ship, and take pictures of it, then you might rent a small warehouse space. Many times instead of using a warehouse space, you could find a small store somewhere in the neighborhood, where there is not a lot of traffic and the landlord is just happy to have the store rented. You might be more comfortable renting that small store, where you will have plenty of light coming in from the window on the street level. You do not have to open it up for public business, and it might give you a very comfortable and spacious place to work in, while you run your eBay business. Remember, while you want your business to grow, you want to do it step-by-step so you do not overburden yourself with any financial constraints that your business might not be able to afford. However, you do want your business to grow; you do want it to grow aggressively because the goal is there, the possibility of earning thousands of dollars, and even earning hundreds of thousands of dollars and more—and it is a very strong possibility while you run your eBay business.

Conclusion

Remember that if you have a store, eBay is also a great way to supplement your store business. If you have a store and decide to auction off some of the merchandise that you carry, you could use it to auction off the slow-moving merchandise and bring in additional revenue, freeing up the money you invested in that merchandise. Then you will be able to expand your business by reinvesting the money that you receive for the slow-moving merchandise into faster moving merchandise. You could also order extra merchandise from your wholesaler and use that merchandise to specifically auction off on eBay and generate income that way.

Another way to also to allow eBay to help your store business to grow, is by listing that you own a store, in your auction description. Give the address of the store, or the location and then people can come to the store and once they are there, they might buy the merchandise that you looking to auction, or they might buy additional merchandise. Say you are auctioning off a piano and people see your auction and that you actually have a store, so people who are interested in that piano or other types of pianos, will want to come to your store to see what you carry.

In addition, in all of your correspondence, when people send you inquiries and you respond to those inquiries, or people actually purchase merchandise from you, let them know about your store and if you are a wholesaler or manufacturer, let them know *that*. No matter what size the auction is for, whether it is for 1,000 or 10,000 units, let people know what type of business you are in because you will never know what else they might buy from you and you do not know who else they might refer to you. Even if they are not in the market to purchase a large quantity of the merchandise that you sell, they might know someone who is looking for that merchandise at a quantity that would make you very happy to sell.

Say you are a manufacturer of certain merchandise and you go ahead and put that merchandise up for sale on eBay. You might say, "Look, you know what? I just put out an auction for a few pieces of ceramics and someone who buys those 3 or 4 pieces of ceramics, there is no way that they could order a hundred pieces from me because they are just an end user." Nevertheless, that end user might own an arts and crafts store or might know someone else who owns a store that would love to carry your merchandise. Say that end user shops at a particular ceramics store and mentions to the owner that they bought some beautiful pieces on eBay and the owner of the store wants to contact you to buy your merchandise. Therefore, it is important in all of your correspondence and on your auctions on eBay to let people know the other options they have to purchase merchandise from you or what other merchandise that you carry and what your business is. This way, you will be able to increase your business and be a step closer to allowing your eBay business to become your full-time business.

I hope you enjoyed this book and I invite you to share your experiences and ideas with me. You can contact me by visiting either of my two sites, www.closeoutexplosion.com or www.DonnyLowy.com

I look forward to hearing from you!

About the Author

Donny Lowy is an experienced entrepreneur and business author whose innovative consulting strategies have helped people start and run profitable online and offline businesses. He is actively involved in the closeout and wholesale business and is a respected expert on doing business on eBay.

If you are ready to start your own eBay business visit
www.closeoutexplosion.com, your source for brand new exclusive closeouts, over-stock, and surplus merchandise priced as low as 80% below wholesale.

For more books, advice, and personal consulting from this author please visit www.DonnyLowy.com

0-595-30674-8

www.ingramcontent.com/pod-product-compliance
Lightning Source LLC
Chambersburg PA
CBHW030742180526
45163CB00003B/893